New France

— six pictorial diaries of people with vision and passion —
with activities, oral, written and creative

a microcosm of the time

Grace Morrison

éditions farandole editions

MAY   2013

Acknowledgements

The author is grateful to the following institutions: the Metropolitan Toronto Public Library; the Marguerite Bourgeoys Museum, Montréal; the Congrégation de Notre-Dame, Montréal; the Centre Culturel Marguerite Bourgeoys, Troyes, France; the Musée des Hospitalières de l'Hôtel-Dieu de Montréal; Sainte-Marie-Among-the-Hurons, Midland, Ontario; the Canadian Canoe Museum, Peterborough, Ontario; the Acadian Centre, Grand Pré, Nova Scotia; the Bibliothèque Nationale, Brussels, Belgium.

Original artwork for the cover design by Elaine Morrison, Jerusalem and Toronto.

Picture Credits
   Metropolitan Toronto Public Library
   National Museums of Canada
   Provincial Archives of Nova Scotia
   John Ross Robertson Collection, Metropolitan Toronto Public Library
   The bark canoes and skin boats of North America, Adney and Chapelle, 36
   Government of Ontario Art Collection, 38
   Dan Fell, Toronto, 59, 201
   The Glory of the Page, Glasgow University, 65, 103, 115
   © Ron Hunt, Midland, Ontario, 77
   Midland Photo Supplies, Midland, Ontario, 85
   Collin Goldie and Ken Mayer, Vancouver, B.C., per Royal Ontario Museum, 99
   Public Archives of Canada © 14360, 111; © 10688, 121, 156; © 13325, 171
   F. Delorme, Congrégation de Notre-Dame, Montréal, 113, 123
   Centre Culturel Marguerite Bourgeoys, Troyes, France, 117
   Gale Research Company, Detroit, Michigan, 138, 240
   Confederation Life Collection, 158
   Collections of Marius Barbeau, 167
   Statue by Hébert, Quebec, 199
   Collin Gillies, Toronto, 212
   Lewis Parker per Parks Canada, 232
   Wine-Art, Toronto, 238

Every effort has been made to contact the sources of the illustrations in this work. If, by chance, someone's name has been omitted, please inform the author.

Design by éditions farandole editions, Glasgow and Toronto
Computer services by Cheryl Rainfield, Toronto
ISBN-13 978-0-9687042-0-2

CANADIAN CATALOGUING IN PUBLICATION DATA
   Morrison, Grace
   New France: six pictorial diaries of people with vision and passion: with activities, oral, written and creative: a microcosm of the time
   Includes bibliographical references and index. ISBN: 0-9687042-0-4
   1. Canada – History – To 1763 (New France). 2. Canada – History – To 1763 (New France) – Biography.
   3. Canada – History – To 1763 (New France) – Problems, exercises, etc. 1. Title.
   FC305.M66 2000   971.01   C00-930920-9
   F1030.M84 2000

Contents

...for Carol and Elaine

Étienne Brûlé

C.W. JEFFERYS

Cahiagué sur la Mer douce,
le 18 juin 1620

Hello there, my Friends!

My name is Étienne Brûlé, and I am going to tell you my story. You are going to be my companions and confidants as we spend this time together. There will be adventure all around us. We shall be the first white people to go down the Rapides de Saint-Louis, to gaze at the magnificent lakes Huron, Ontario, Érie and Superior, and to travel the full length of the Susquehanna River. We shall be Samuel de Champlain's interpreters, spending twenty-three years with the Hurons! In fact, we might well be called the first coureurs de bois on this vast continent.

So, off we go!

Étienne Brûlé

Étienne Brûlé

1591-1633

Hi, there! Come nearer, my friends; I want to speak to you. My name is Étienne Brûlé. The year is 1608 and I'm barely 17 when adventure strikes me as lightning strikes a tree. My imagination is fired. My real name is Brusle, as the missionaries were to write it later in their *Jesuit Relations* or reports. My parents are simple farming folk who live in Île-de-France, just south of Paris.

I had learned that my hero, Samuel de Champlain, the famous explorer, was equipping a ship to sail to New France. All those marvellous stories that I had heard about this new land far across the sea had made my head spin. So, off I went to the port of Honfleur, ready to set sail for that unknown land where a bold and fascinating life awaited me. Oh, the dreams I had! I thought about the fishermen from Spain, England, Portugal and France setting out for the Grand Banks. I imagined I was Jacques Cartier on his long journey in 1534. I envied Samuel de Champlain, Sieur de Monts, Pontgravé, and all the other heroes of the time. I wanted to follow in their footsteps, and throw myself headlong into adventure — the discovery of new lands!

Now, imagine a dark and dank little boat pitching and rolling on a swelling sea. Put me on board for what seemed like an eternity — 10 long weeks — with rough company and seasickness.

Being on the open sea was a new experience for me. I wondered if my choice had been the right one. However, gradually conditions improved. As we drew closer to the Grand Banks, whales, dolphins and schools of fish started appearing and swimming alongside us. It was beautiful. We did some good fishing, and dropped anchor at last at Tadoussac on the Saguenay River, a fine waterway if ever there was one.

Sauvages![*] Look, my friends, it's the first time we have seen *Sauvages*! Look at *him* over there, handsome and proud as he eases his way towards us in the water. He handles his birchbark canoe with masterly skill. He's friendly, strong and at ease, his wife by his side, his companions behind. What an impressive picture! As I gaze on him, I'm filled with a longing to know the joys and pleasures of nature. And how beautiful his wife is! Her olive-coloured skin, her long, black, silken hair and her beaded glass ornaments attract and fascinate me.

War drums! Forget your seductive dreams, Brusle! It is Iroquois against Montagnais: it's 1610 and the fur trade is being threatened. The English and Dutch are supporting the Iroquois, who have become our enemies. We *Français* set out to do battle. Paddle, my friends, as fast as you can, to the Richelieu River — the *rivière des Iroquois*. Look, there are easily 100 of them, armed! Shouts, chants, dancing, rhythm upon rhythm, all day and all night...till dawn. The battle's on! What do I see around me? The arquebus readied, the bow tautened, terror growing, blood flowing. Shrieks and shouts echo through the forest as the victors hunt the vanquished. Then,

---

[*] The French word *Sauvages* was used in a good way, my friends, meaning "those who lived in freedom, those who were the friends of nature." I was told that *sauvages* has a Latin root, *silva*, meaning a "woodland."

there is silence — nothing at all. It's over, it's done.

"Monsieur de Champlain, I want to go and live with the *Sauvages*. I want to share their way of life, their customs, their exploits and passions."

"I understand what you are saying, Brusle. Actually, I need a bold sort of lad to travel around with the Hurons, to explore their rivers and lakes, and to find out more about these copper mines everyone is talking about. Yes, I would like you to go with them. My friend, the Algonquin chief Iroquet and I have formed an alliance. A young Huron, Savignon, will be exchanged for you for the duration of the winter months. I shall take Savignon back to France with me while you stay with Iroquet and his people. This way you will become acquainted with their language and customs, their lands and waterways. You will be the first white man ever to do anything like this here, and you will be paid for it."

"I accept, Sir!"

That is how I came to spend winter and spring with my new friends. I was happy to be with them, joyful to share each moment of their lives. I voyaged to what seemed like the end of the world, along the lengths of the Ottawa River and the French River — the Rivière des Français — right to that great freshwater "sea" you call Lake Huron. I heard the thundering noise of falling water over the Chutes de la Chaudière. I felt the curling, frothing water of the Rapides de Saint-Louis under my canoe. I ran, I danced, I went to bed at sundown and rose at sunrise. Nature had become my companion, my friends, and I drank in everything she had to offer. I drank thirstily, and I loved it.

It was June, 1611. We were at the Rapides de Saint-Louis. Dressed like my friends, the *Sauvages*, I met M. de Champlain and told him what I had learned in the last months. My mind and my mouth were replying to his questions, but my heart was saying: "It's with the Hurons that you must spend the rest of your life. What do you have in common with the officers and missionaries in Québec,* after such an incredible experience? You know what your fate is now and where it lies." And that's true, I did know it. I went back to live with the *Sauvages*.

The years passed. I now knew the Huron language like my own, as M. de Champlain had intended. I was interpreter for the Récollet and Jesuit missionaries and the merchants. My home became that piece of land, that peninsula that juts out into the *Mer douce* (I believe you call it Georgian Bay in your time). There were 30,000 *Sauvages* there who treated me like their brother. I didn't know then that I was going to spend 23 years there.

The capital of our territory was Cahiagué, where there were 200 longhouses — *longues cabanes* — made of wood. There were about 40 people living in each house — 8,000 in total: this was one of the most populated Native settlements north of Mexico.

"Hey! Over here, pass me the ball! No, wait! Now throw it, throw it! Look out, behind you! Ugh, missed again!" I loved that great game, lacrosse! There were 100 men on each side; the field was about a mile* long. And what a din! It was great to run around almost naked in the warm

---

*The word *Québec* comes from the *kebec*, the name the Native peoples of the area gave to this place where the river narrowed. M. de Champlain liked the name. To Jacques Cartier it had been the Iroquoian village of Stadacona, 70 years earlier.

* As you know, one of our miles is the same as 1.6 km in your day.

September sun. We played and played for days without a thought of the morrow.

We also prayed, prayed to the spirits, the okis, the manitous who were in the trees, the lakes, the animals... And we listened to the shamans and respected their magical powers.

War, once more — Hurons against Iroquois! It was 1615. Samuel de Champlain, bold and sure of himself, had kept his word: just as he had promised, he led our warriors on an attack on the Iroquois capital, Onondaga, on the south shore of Lake Ontario. I travelled to the Andastes nation, an ally of the Hurons, to seek extra help. It was a long journey, but I succeeded; I brought back 500 men with me. However, by the time we had arrived at Onondaga, the battle had been lost. My Huron friends, badly prepared and poorly disciplined as they were, had fought an enemy that was ten times more skillful and warlike than they were. As far as I was concerned, that day was the beginning of the end of the Huron people.

You know that I was well and truly blamed for my late arrival at Onondaga that day. But it wasn't my fault! We had 29 miles of portage before reaching the mouth of the river at Lake Ontario, and then we had to head south through forests and swampland. It wasn't my fault we were late. The battle had been lost by the time we had arrived at Onondaga.

But what beautiful lands there were to explore! I went all the way down the Susquehanna River to the sea, to Chesapeake Bay — 500 miles. There was wildlife everywhere, and the weather was so warm! I was the first white man to make this marvellous journey. My canoe was my constant companion.

However, the fury of war was never far away. I had to pass through Seneca country on my way home. It proved dangerous country for me; I was seized and put to the torture. Even today, my friends, as I speak, I can feel the flames licking at my skin. I can still see those black clouds in the distance, forerunners of a storm, just as I did that day. They gave me an idea, an idea I had to grasp quickly.

"Those clouds are a sign of divine anger!" I shouted out in as powerful a voice as I could find. "God himself has come to put a curse on your whole race!" The Chief believed me. I was untied, I was freed! I know that I had used my cunning, but what would you have done in a similar situation? *Ah, la peau de Brusle brûlait!*

I had almost recovered when I met up with Samuel de Champlain again in 1618 at the large settlement of Trois-Rivières. He commissioned me to go in search of the *Grand lac*, Lake Superior in your day, to be found on the other side of the great rapids from Lake Huron. I said I would do it. That summer, I crossed the *Grand lac* from east to west. It was like a sea to me; I plunged my paddle into it with gusto. Of course I didn't write down anything about it, as I didn't write about anything I did. Words were *living* things for me, not marks that you put down laboriously on parchment — let others do that task! I know I was the first white man to see and to explore four of these five marvels of our world, the Great Lakes! Give me my 100 pistoles[*] a year and my life of adventure, and I'll be happy!

The year is 1629, and lo and behold, New France is in English hands! Admiral Kirke took

---

[*] The pistole was one of our coins. It was used in France and Spain as well as in New France. It was made of gold, and had a value that varied.

Québec and captured Samuel de Champlain at the same time. People said I'd betrayed the *Français* because I'd piloted the English ships up the St. Lawrence River. But did I have a choice? I was a prisoner of the English, and I realized very quickly who would be the victor and who the vanquished. The *Français* didn't have a chance that time around.

Things were soon to change, however. In 1632, New France was in French hands once again, thanks to the decision of King Charles I of England, who needed money to fill his coffers. He sold this half of a continent, this New France that we had known, back to the *Français* for a ridiculously small sum. And who came back as the governor? Sieur de Champlain.

As for me, if I was no longer considered a good *Français*, I certainly wasn't a great friend of the English either! Even my Huron brothers turned against me. Was it because they thought I was a traitor? I don't know the reason. All I know is this: one beautiful day in June, 1633, my Hurons took me, tortured me and put me to death. They had been my brothers and sisters, my loves, my passions and my life for 23 years. With them I had known the forests, lakes, rivers and falls I loved so much. You see, I had an extraordinary and fantastic life! Perhaps I was the first coureur de bois.... *Adieu, et bonne chance!*

A coureur de bois

Le coureur de bois

What is a coureur de bois? In the seventeenth century, young Frenchmen like me travelled to the Native villages of New France to barter for furs. As far as I'm concerned the coureurs de bois played an important role in the history of New France. The skins they brought back had great commercial value, of course. But, over and above, these young men formed a close bond between the Native peoples and the French colonists. There were some priests, administrators, and even pioneers who turned up their noses when this way of life was mentioned, but the coureurs de bois would never have traded their lifestyle for the others'. Dressed comfortably in animal skins, they canoed over vast distances, sometimes staying away from base for two years or more. They would come back to Montréal loaded down with furs, happy to get their money or merchandise from the merchants. It was a great life!

a)   Take on the roles of two coureurs de bois who have just arrived at an important Native settlement. They speak a little Huron, or the Native peoples speak a little French. Prepare a skit, rehearse it and present it to the class.

b)   Samuel de Champlain has asked for a report on our latest meeting with the Native peoples. Reply to him in a clear, simple style, commenting on the welcome we received and the way of life we observed. Try to write your report using calligraphy, as it was done at that time.

c)   Clothes must be suitable for the person in his or her particular environment. (You can think about sports, for example, or any activity out of doors.) Write two paragraphs about this thought, and illustrate your ideas with drawings.

d)   Would you like to have been coureurs de bois, my friends? Imagine you have chosen this way of life with all its risks and adventures. Your families can't understand your decisions. You leave home and head for the St. Lawrence River. Before leaving, you write letters to your parents where you try to persuade them to think differently. Use some good arguments. Good luck!

We've just been discussing the life of the coureurs de bois, and I have to confess that it's a way of life that would have suited me perfectly. It would have been just right for me physically, using up my energy, allowing me to live with nature — and I love nature — offering me an outlet for my passion for life, my love of adventure and my strong, determined streak. Indeed, I myself played a fundamental role in the drama of the fur trade, as I was a link between the Native peoples and the merchants who paid me an annual salary of 100 pistoles to encourage the Native population to come and trade. I had learned the language and customs of the Hurons well, as had been Samuel de Champlain's plan from the outset. Perhaps he was not too keen that I used this knowledge for the benefit of the merchants as well as for that of the missionaries. Who knows?

Anyway, now that we have set the scene in the framework of New France in the seventeenth century, we're going to speak about the places, actions and events that will allow you and me to have marvellous dreams — wonderful dreams! We're now going to live through unforgettable times!

The Holroyd. *An important violin* by Antonio Stradivari, Cremona, 1727

Violins

What did we bring to New France? Not much in the way of material things, that's for sure. We young, carefree, adventurous types didn't have many possessions, but we did bring our traditions and customs, and whatever knowledge we had. And we brought our songs, stories and dances!

If your imagination is active enough (and I know it is), you can hear the fiddle music and feel the dance beat. So, let's join in!

a)   Folk music is a very important part of the culture of a country. In a group of four, find some examples of folk music. Prepare a little commentary on the content and form of the music. Give a presentation to the class.

b)   Compose a tune for people to dance to — any kind of dance. Play it on instruments if you can, and have a great and lively time with your friends.

c)   Consider the French words *violoniste* and *violoneux*. Look up their definitions in a dictionary. Compare the meanings of the two words, noting how they differ from one another and how they resemble one another. Draw two sketches to illustrate the different situations where you would be either a *violoniste* or a *violoneux*.

d)   You have most probably heard of Stradivarius, the maker of wonderful stringed instruments. Try to find the names of other famous stringed instrument makers. Find out more about this marvel of handmade objects, the violin, this mix of science and artistry.

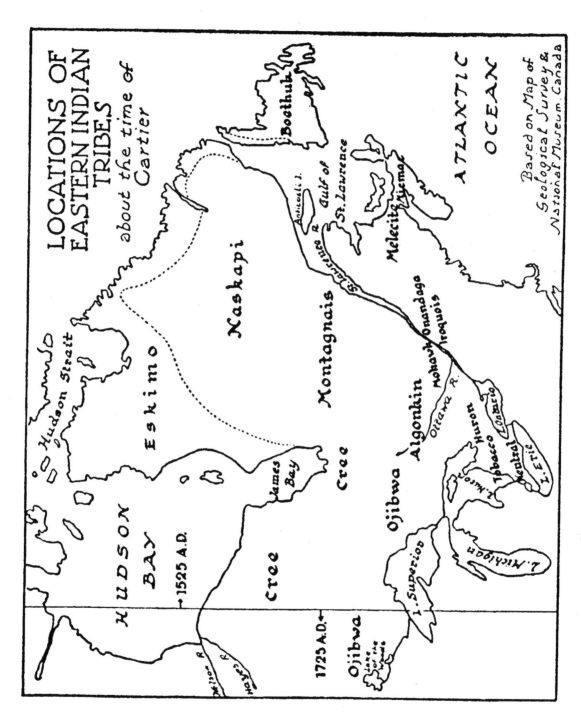

Locations of Eastern Indian Tribes

The Beginning of the Seventeenth Century

In truth, dancing and singing played a large role in our life in New France, as it did in many other parts of the world at that time. In our mother country, France, Louis XIII le Juste was on the throne. His reign lasted from 1610-1643. There were many troubles during that period: the assassination of Concini and a new religious war, to name but two. The uprisings of the *Grands* of the State — which we called the *Fronde* — were to follow in 1648-1652. In spite of the intrigues of the Queen Mother, Louis XIII finished up by handing over the power to Cardinal Richelieu. The country then got embroiled in the Thirty Years War. The King died in 1643.

a) Look up information about the history of other countries during the years 1600-1650. Categorize the information under the headings: country, type of government, religion, wars, natural disasters, inventions explorations.

b) Imagine that the year is 1608, and that you are accompanying me on a French vessel en route for New France. Right from the first day of the voyage till our arrival in Tadoussac you keep a journal. You write down everything that you find interesting. The weather is fine, the sea is calm. You're sitting comfortably up on deck, writing. Don't forget to mention your pal Brusle!

c) I love maps! How about you? Try to find some maps of my time (or at least good reproductions). Compare them to the maps of your century, then draw an old-style map of an imaginary land: be precise, give topographical details, indicate the scale, and don't forget the compass points and the legend. Give your land a name, an interesting one!

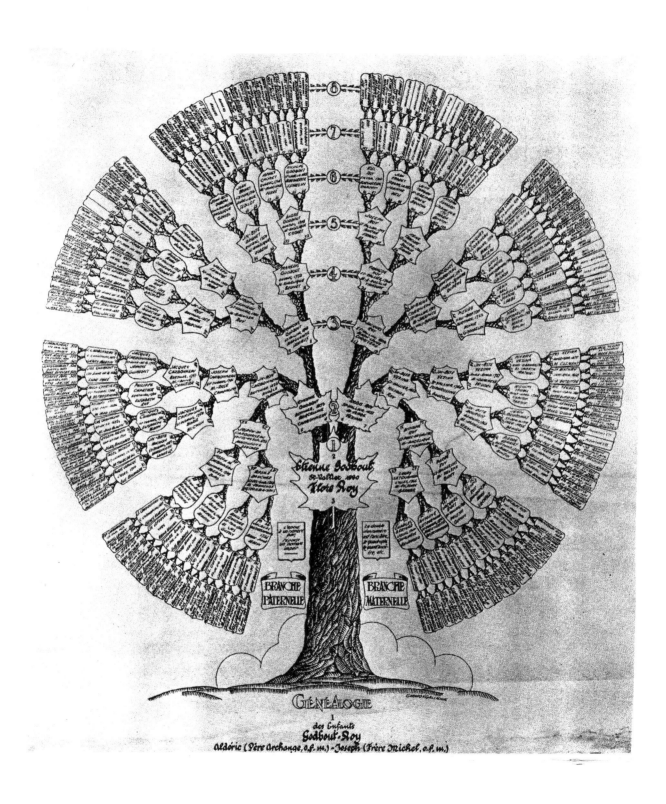

GÉNÉALOGIE

des Enfants

Godbout-Roy

Aldéric (Père Archange, o.f.m.) - Joseph (Frère Michel, o.f.m.)

Names

I think my name is an interesting one. It is written as *Brûlé* in your century, but it was *Brusle* at the beginning of the seventeenth century. *Étienne* was *Estienne*. Often in French, when the letter *s* is dropped from a word, it is replaced by an accent; that's what happened in my case. An acute accent was added at the end, probably to make the sound stronger. You can see how the spelling of a name can change through the years; it can also vary from place to place.

a)   Draw your family tree. Pay close attention to the names. Have some of them changed, and if so, why? For cultural, social, religious or political reasons?

b)   Do you have a nickname? What is it? Why do you have it? Choose three names you could give me, always keeping in mind my fine qualities of course. Write down your choices and discuss them with your group members who have done the same.

c)   New France was an easy name to invent. Become explorers who crisscross the oceans and continents, and space too; why not? Write a skit in which you "discover" a country or planet. Rehearse the scene, choosing your dialogue carefully. Give an accurate description of your "discovery" and your means of transportation. Name this place, according to how you and your friends react to it.

Samuel de Champlain at Québec

Samuel de Champlain
c.1567 - 1635

Sieur de Champlain, my boss, is one of the most famous explorers of the seventeenth century. He was my great hero! Like him, I had a passion for the discovery of unknown lands. He was an excellent cartographer; some of his maps still exist in your time. After his first voyage in 1603 to this land soon to be known as New France, he succeeded in persuading Henri IV, King of France, to establish a colony. In 1608 he founded Québec. In 1620 he was named to the post of lieutenant-governor, and in 1633 he became Governor Champlain. He knew how to forge a friendly relationship with the Hurons, who came to look on him as a *grand chef*. As a religious man and a true believer, he could and did win the support of the Church.

a)   Do some research on Samuel de Champlain. Create a project on his explorations, maps, way of life, and relationships with the Church, the French merchants, and the Native peoples. Present your project to the class.

b)   Write a poem which tells of an exploration — a journey to the moon if you want to, if you can imagine it. Then choose a piece of music that will help to give the right atmosphere. Recite your work with the music in the background, and lower the lights. Here you are, an artist!

c)   Recreate the first meeting between Samuel de Champlain and me, Étienne Brûlé — or Brusle, as he called me. With a friend, rehearse the roles and present your skit to the class. (Try to bring our similarities as well as our differences.)

LIBRO SEGVN
DO DE LA MAR, Y SVS MOVI
MIENTOS. Y COMO FVE
INVENTADA LA NA
VEGACION .:.

The Sea

The sea can be a barrier, a frontier or a link. From ancient times, people have been fascinated by the sea and by what's beyond it. They have built boats of all sorts to help them explore the world around them. It's human nature to try to discover what there is in the unknown. In your day, people travel into space, I hear. I find that idea fascinating!

a) Find some information on ancient boats. Try to discover at least four different types. You will find that a good illustrated dictionary can be an excellent help. Draw the boats; below each one, write a paragraph explaining its structure, dimensions, use and country of origin.

b) Do you like the sea? I love it. Imagine an underwater expedition in diving gear, or in a submarine or bathyscaphe — all these marvellous inventions you have in your century. What do you see? What are you looking for? Describe the world around you. You are now an underwater explorer like Jacques Cousteau in your time.

c) The fishermen of my time knew the Grand Banks well. Where are the Grand Banks? Where did these fishermen come from? Their voyages were long. Do some research on them, and go back even farther to the ancient voyages, to those of Ulysses, Sinbad, the Celts and the Vikings for example. Now make a presentation to the class, using maps of course. This is an exciting project!

Iroquois longhouses. The Iroquois called themselves the "Ho-de-no-sau-nee" or "people of the longhouse."
The longhouse was a universal dwelling among the Iroquois tribes. Usually, two or more families
lived in each longhouse. Their quarters were separated by walls or hanging furs.

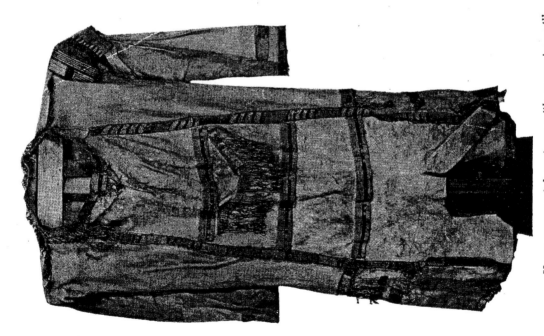

*Huron ceremonial costume with porcupine-quill
and deer-hoof trimmings, at Ashmolean Museum,
Oxford. (Tradescant Collection, 1656.)*

The Native Peoples

Let's go from the seas to the rivers, great and small...to the canoes...to the Native peoples. Ah, the Indigenous peoples — my friends for more than 23 years and, in the end, my judges! The stamina, the beauty, the wisdom of the Hurons had always attracted me to them. The Hurons and the Algonquins got along well together. The Iroquois, on the other hand, united in its League of the Five Nations — Mohawk, Seneca, Cayuga, Oneida and Onondaga — were their enemies. The League of the Five Nations had been a fine, democratic idea put forward by Dekanawida in the 1400s. Now of course, in my century, there were other alliances to add to that one. The alliance between the French and the Hurons was a solid one and a profitable one for business, as was the alliance between the English, Dutch and the Iroquois. In the beginning it was the colonists who helped their Native allies in their wars; when war broke out between the English and French, the opposite happened.

a) Locate the Huron settlements on a map showing the Native peoples' territories in the seventeenth century. Our area extended from the *Mer douce* — called Georgian Bay in your time — right to Lake Ontario. Are there still some traces of our people there today? Where? Find out about Sainte-Marie-des-Hurons.* If you can, go and visit this site of the former Jesuit mission in New France. It was the biggest Jesuit establishment north of Mexico.

b) Make a maquette of a longhouse, which was our typical type of dwelling. (You will find some illustrations in encyclopedias, dictionaries and books on the Native peoples.) Write a paragraph about each of its different parts. Label each part of the maquette to match its description.

c) Like us, the Native peoples had numerous legends about their way of life, their religions and their beliefs. You are now going to create one. Let your imagination soar! You are a Huron man seated near the fire in your longhouse, or a Huron woman interrupting her domestic chores for a story or a dream. Your family and friends gather around. Everything is quiet and dark. The smoke is snaking out of the hole in the roof. You begin to speak....

---

* The address is: Saint-Marie-au-pays-des-Hurons; Huronia Historic Park, P.O. Box 160, Midland, Ontario L4R 4K8 telephone: (705) 526-7838

C'EST L'AVIRON
qui nous mène en haut

(Folklore)

1. M'en re-ve-nant de la jo-lie Ro-chel-le,
2. J'ai ren-con-tré trois jo-lies de-moi-sel-les;

M'en re-ve-nant de la jo-lie Ro-chel-le, J'ai ren-con-
J'ai ren-con-tré trois jo-lies de-moi-sel-les; J'ai point choi-

REFRAIN

tré trois jo-lies de-moi-sel-les. C'est l'a-vi-ron qui nous
si, mais j'ai pris la plus bel-le.

mè-ne, qui nous mè-ne, C'est l'a-vi-ron qui nous mène en haut.

2. J'ai rencontré trois jolies demoiselles;]2
   J'ai point choisi, mais j'ai pris la plus belle.

3. J'ai point choisi, mais j'ai pris la plus belle;]2
   J'l'y fis monter derrièr' moi, sur ma selle.

4. J'l'y fis monter derrièr' moi, sur ma selle;]2
   J'y fis cent lieues sans parler avec elle.

5. J'y fis cent lieues sans parler avec elle;]2
   Au bout d'cent lieues, ell' me d'mandit à boire.

6. Au bout d'cent lieues, ell' me d'mandit à boire;]2
   Je l'ai menée auprès d'une fontaine.

7. Je l'ai menée auprès d'une fontaine;]2
   Quand ell' fut là, ell' ne voulut point boire.

8. Quand ell' fut là, ell' ne voulut point boire;]2
   Je l'ai menée au logis de son père.

9. Je l'ai menée au logis de son père;]2
   Quand ell' fut là, ell' buvait à pleins verres.

10. Quand ell' fut là, ell' buvait à pleins verres;]2
    A la santé de son père et sa mère.

11. A la santé de son père et sa mère;]2
    A la santé de ses soeurs et ses frères.

Songs

Stories from their past made up a very important part of the Native peoples' culture. The French, too, set foot on this unknown land with *their* stories, songs and legends. We gradually adapted our songs to our new life, sometimes changing their words or moods to suit our different environment. For us, the *chansons à répondre et à refrain*, which were rhythmic and repetitious, made our long journeys by canoe seem shorter. They made our paddles beat the water faster as we sang and sang for days on end.

a)   I've often sung the song "M'en revenant de la jolie Rochelle" as I paddled my canoe. Try to sing it with your friends. The tempo — fairly quick — will be measured by the beating of the paddles in the water. Keep it steady, and watch out for splashes!

b)   There are songs written especially to go along with a task or an activity: lullabies, marching songs, harvest songs — and even, why not, drinking songs. Draw up a short list of these indicating the task or activity that goes with each one, and add to that each song's country of origin.

c)   Become composers! Write a simple melody. Play it on instruments if you can. Record it and give the cassette to someone you like. I'll listen to it with interest.

Discussing the pelts

The Fur Trade

The thing that really interested many of my contemporaries in New France was profit! The prime profit maker was the fur trade; there was no doubt about that. Sieur de Monts, one of the companions of Samuel de Champlain, had been granted a monopoly for the trapping of animals and the trading of their furs by Henri IV, King of France. What this meant was that no other country but France had the right to exchange goods for furs. This trade would prove extremely profitable for the French merchants. As I was one of Samuel de Champlain's interpreters — the first one in Huronia, to be honest — I became an important part of this whole enterprise. I was often the middleman between the merchants and the Native peoples.

a) Let's think about this for a moment! Do you think the colony of New France would have been as prosperous as it was without the fur trade? Do you think it would have just eked out an existence without this commercial activity? Write your answers to these questions, paying attention to the aims and objectives of the people involved.

b) Try to find different types of furs (a good encylopedia should provide you with good research material, and maybe a furrier in your neighbourhood can lend you samples of the most common ones). Classify them under the headings: kind of animal, country of origin, climate of that country, vegetation of that country, kind of hair, thickness, colour. Now draw your own conclusions as to the relationship between the animals mentioned and nature.

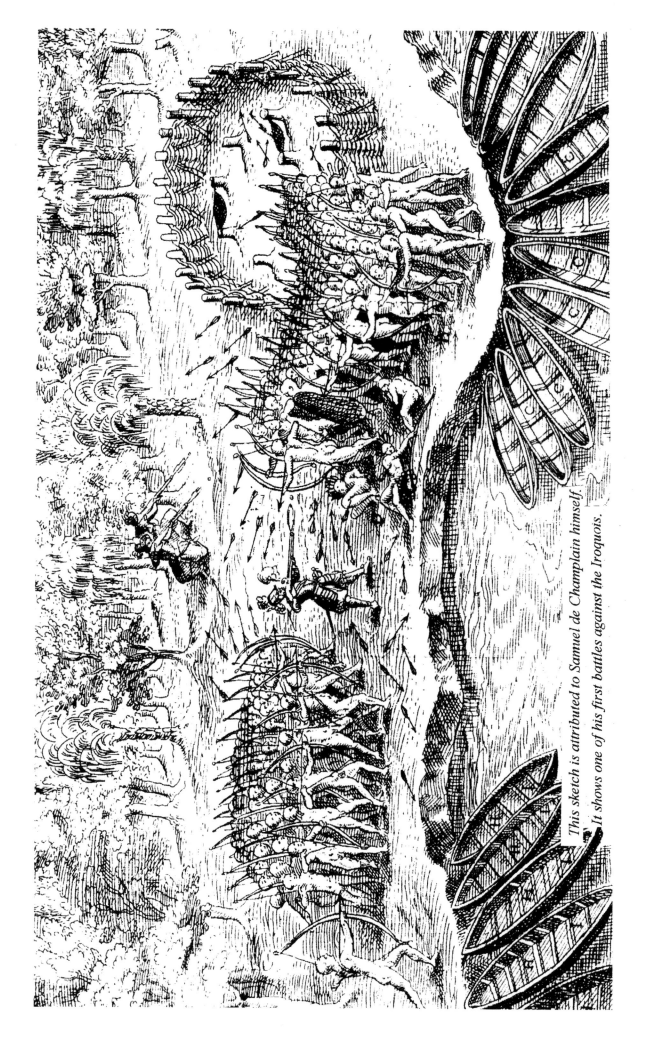

This sketch is attributed to Samuel de Champlain himself.
It shows one of his first battles against the Iroquois.

War

Very often I could predict the outcome of the battles between the Native peoples. The ones in which I was involved were those where my Huron brothers and their French allies were fighting against the Iroquois and their English and Dutch allies. However, the first battle I mention in my opening story is the one between the Montagnais and the Iroquois. In fact, the Montagnais had to seek shelter in our fort during one of these skirmishes. We helped things simmer down — or at least we tried to.

a) Why do you think there were skirmishes, battles and wars between the different bands of Native peoples? Give your answer in written form, and express your opinion about physical combat, generally speaking.

b) I am going to put forward a bold hypothesis: suppose that there could exist a world without war; consider the situation, and think about the advantages and disadvantages if any. Prepare a debate with a friend who does not share your point of view. Keep in mind war's social, financial and religious aspects.

c) For a long, long time man has used dreadful weapons and machines to fight his fellow human beings. Find out about weapons from different times and civilizations, and classify them using the headings: power, size, shape, material used, individual or collective weapon, country of origin, use. You can use drawings or sketches to illustrate your work.

CARTE DE LA NOUVELLE-FRANCE AU 17ᵐᵉ SIÈCLE.

The First Voyages

Although wars had often held me in their grasp, there was still enough energy in me for my two favourite occupations, the two passions that had guided me through life: adventure — *la folle aventure* — and exploration! During my first stay with Chief Iroquet, I went up the Ottawa River — the Rivière des Outaouais — to Lake Huron. The Ottawa River was a natural line of communication between the Native peoples of the east and west.

The Native peoples settled in the area of *Kitche-Sippi* — the *grande rivière* — the Ottawa River. For the first colonists who wanted to travel from the St. Lawrence River to the Great Lakes, the *grande rivière* was a natural passageway. The Algonquins lived along its banks, and so they gave it their name. The Outaouais, another people in the area, travelled down it to get to Montréal: it was the Outaouais who gave it the name you know today — the Ottawa River.

a) Follow my journey from Québec to the *Mer douce*, or that "freshwater sea" you call Georgian Bay. Trace out this route on a map, underlining the most interesting places along the way.

b) What similarities and differences would you find if *you* undertook the same voyage with some friends in your century? What mode of transportation would you choose? Write an account of the journey, and don't forget to describe the relief, climate, fauna and flora, population and natural resources of the area you cover. *Bon voyage!*

c) Where are the Rapides de Saint-Louis? They are near your large city of Montréal, but they don't have the same name as they did in my time. Try to imagine my feelings as I am about to shoot them in my canoe — the first white man to do so. Assume my role, create a text, rehearse it and present it to the class.

This is a song of the Medicine Men's Society, one of the most exciting of the Iroquois ceremonies. Of it Dr. William N. Fenton wrote: "The songs of twelve to fifteen men shaking gourd rattles in unison fill the narrow confines of a log house to overflowing, and in the overtones one hears the cries of mystic animals that were the familiars of past generations of shamans."

Chief Joseph Logan of the Six Nations Reserve in Ontario sang the ceremonial songs for Dr. Fenton in 1941. Chief Logan said that the Medicine Society is descended from an old society of shamans, or medicine men. When a member or a sick person wants a feast to be held, he asks a member of the opposite half of the tribe to conduct the ceremony. The first part of the ceremony is called "throwing in a song" when the medicine men from the leading side sing in turn. Then the conductor hands over the fire to the leader of the sponsor's side and his men sing individually. Then follows the main part of the ritual when all join in the songs of the Medicine Dance. The songs run in pairs and there are forty-four of them, the actual dancing beginning with the twentieth.

The song given here is one of the "throwing songs," and its "running wolf" theme is a favorite, turning up in several Iroquois rituals. Literally it goes:

Hothayonii ha'adakee gahentenshon hadakee
Male wolf runs on the open fields he runs

WOLF SONG

The Missionaries

The coureurs de bois were not the only ones to explore new territories. Jesuit and Récollet missionaries arrived in New France as soon as Samuel de Champlain decided to Christianize the Native peoples. I often acted as interpreter for these missionaries, and I helped them edit their dictionary of the Huron language. In fact, I was the intermediary between them and my Native brothers. Perhaps they wouldn't have been accepted into Huronia so readily if I hadn't been there. I know that they did not care for my kind of lifestyle (even M. de Champlain, in an ungrateful mood, was to refer to me later as *fort vicieux, et adonné aux femmes*), but after all, it's each man for himself in a hostile environment, each woman too!

a) Written in the royal commission given by Henri IV, King of France, you can find three main points which were essential to the colonization of New France. These points are: the riches of the territory, the conversion of the Native peoples, and the fur trade. Say what you think about these three points, paying particular attention to the second one. Prepare an account on this topic, and present it to the class.

b) Do some research on Father Brébeuf, written also as Brébœuf, and Father Lalemant, written as L'Alemant in my time. (Be careful, as there is more than one Lalemant!) What happened to these missionaries? How could they possibly deserve such a fate? Can you find an explanation for their tragic end? Write a small report on their deaths, and the possible reasons for them.

c) As you know or can guess — because every people has its religion or at least its beliefs — the Hurons had their own religion. They recognized the spirits, the okis, the manitous which they found in nature. For them, as for numerous other peoples, every natural thing had a soul. I myself accepted these ancient beliefs, at least to a certain point. Learn about different religions — from the West, from the East, from all over that magnificent world that is yours. Draw up a list of their principle doctrines, their taboos (or what is forbidden), their sacred works, their various religious practices. Which religion would you like to embrace? Why?

Lacrosse was played with a hundred players a side

The Games

Just as we loved our spirits, we loved our games, our sports. They were more like battles sometimes, they were so fierce. In fact, two of your most popular national sports were invented by the Native peoples. The one I preferred was the *jeu de la crosse*, also called the *jeu de crosse* — "lacrosse" in your day. It didn't have quite the same rules as it does in your century, but it had the same objectives: to play as well as possible, and to win!

a)   Organize a game of lacrosse with your friends. Study the rules of the game. We didn't have many rules, and some of our games became a little rough — to the point of a few cracked skulls! Be careful then, and play with a sporting spirit. You can name your teams after the Native peoples.

b)   You will probably have guessed that our teams and our playing field were quite different from yours. Imagine you are attending one of our games, and are taking notes on the similarities and the differences between our way of playing and yours. Pay particular attention to the equipment, dress, ground, rules, and number of players involved. We used a small, hard knot of wood for a ball, which we carried in a curved stick with a net made of gut at one end. The games could be long, lasting all day or going on for several days. Sometimes up to 200 players took part. Write your notes clearly; I shall be interested in looking at any sketches you make to go with them.

c)   Hockey, too, comes from the Native peoples. All our players needed were a curved stick and a knot from a tree. I find the origins of sports really fascinating. Find out the history of several sports, noting that the players used what they found in their environment for equipment or material, and that they had to adapt to the lay of the land for their playing field. Do a mini-project on this, using drawings, diagrams, and old pictures.

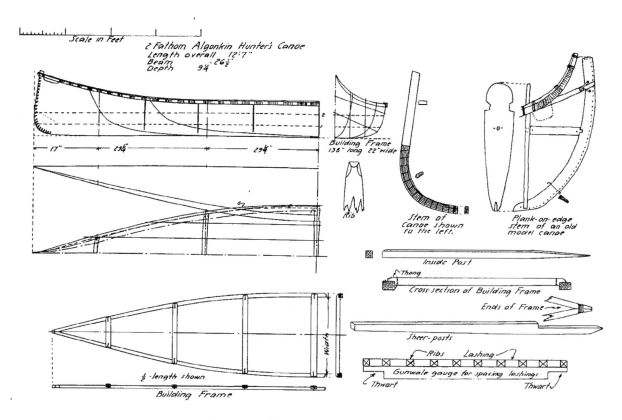

ALGONKIN, 2-FATHOM HUNTER'S CANOE, without headboards. Details of building frame, stakes or posts, gauge, and stem.

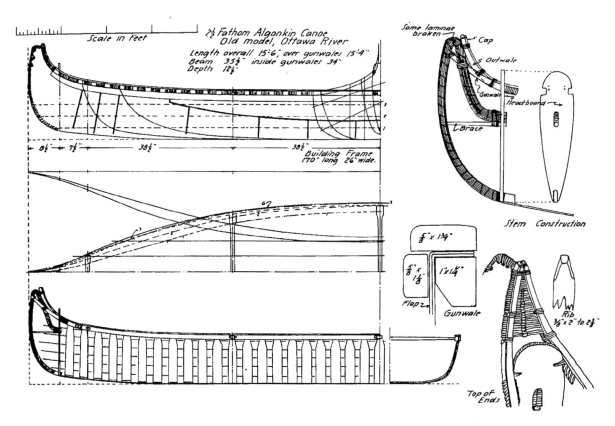

OLD MODEL, OTTAWA RIVER, ALGONKIN CANOE, combining capacity with easy paddling qualities.

The Canoe

Enough playing, my friends! There are canoes to be built, birchbark canoes light enough for the portages and strong enough for the rapids.

a) You have become an expert in the construction of canoes.* In front of you is a class full of apprentices ready and eager to learn your art. Read about it. With the help of a series of drawings that are as detailed as possible, you are going to give your apprentices a fascinating lesson on the art of canoe-building, right from the choice of the tree to the canoe's gliding into the river.

b) Imagine the Huronia of my time without birch trees. What changes would that have brought about? You are a journalist. Write a short article on this topic, with drawings of course, for the illustrated magazine *My Friends From the Past*. Be careful with the vocabulary you use because this magazine is widely read.

c) You are the captain of the best rowing team on the *Mer douce*. This area of water appears as Georgian Bay in your atlas. You've decided to challenge all the teams of the area to a race. Create a publicity campaign to advertise this event so that all the neighbouring villages will be informed. You will have hundreds of spectators. Off you go! *Bonne chance!*

---

* Did you know that the French fathom or *brasse* was the length from one fingertip to the other of your outstretched arms? This length varied, of course, but was roughly 1.6 m, whereas the English fathom is about 1.8 m.

Try to arrange a trip to a special place that exists in your time:
    The Canadian Canoe Museum
    910 Monaghan Road
    Peterborough, Ontario K9J 7F4
    tel: (705) 748-9153   internet site: canoemuseum.net

I'm sure you will enjoy it!

Étienne Brûlé at the mouth of the Humber River, site of the city of Toronto

The Journeys to the South

Without a canoe, my explorations would have been impossible, of course. For me, the canoe was a practical means of transportation; it was easy to handle, and quick to become a real extension of my own lithe and supple body. Every instrument — whether it be for work, play or art — has to be an extension of the self to be well used. I know I was the first *Français* to make long journeys to the south, to explore new territories and return safe and sound. All this I did by canoe.

a)   Follow my route from my home beside the *Mer douce* to Onondaga on the south shore of Lake Ontario. Then accompany me down the Susquehanna River: have courage and patience, because we have more than 500 miles to travel! Draw a map of these journeys, indicating everything I mention in my story. Don't forget the scale, the legend and the compass points.

b)   Since you are my companion for the voyage and you write better than I do, you have to keep the log for the journey to Onondaga. Be precise in your recordings. Begin with the 29 miles of portage to reach the mouth of the river. (They tell me there's a big city there in your century. What's it called?)

c)   What kind of wildlife would we find as we travelled down the Susquehanna River? Create an artistic collage using pictures of the fauna and flora of the areas we covered.

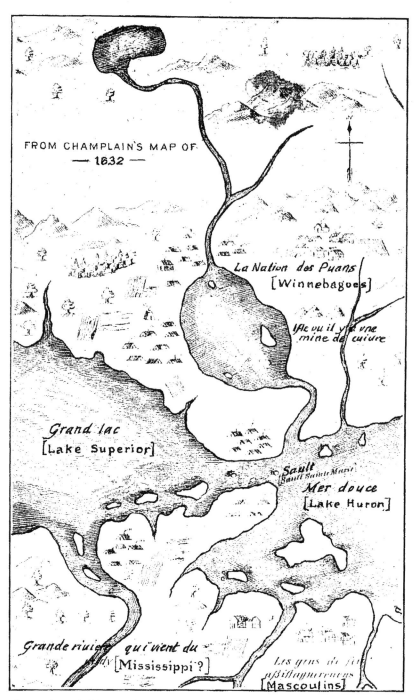

FROM CHAMPLAIN'S MAP OF
— 1632 —

La Nation des Puans
[Winnebagoes]

Isle ou il y a vne
mine de cuivre

Grand lac
[Lake Superior]

Sault
[Sault Sainte Marie]

Mer douce
[Lake Huron]

Grande riuiere qui vient du
[Mississippi ?]

Les gens de feu
assistaguerrons
[Mascoulins]

*A portion of Champlain's map of 1632, from information supplied by
Étienne Brûlé.*

The Lakes

The Susquehanna River was long and beautiful. I enjoyed its scenery. It was different from anything I'd seen before. However, it's when I saw Lake Superior for the first time that I was struck by the grandeur and power of nature. *Our* name for this lake was the *Grand lac*. I scanned the horizon, and all I could see was water, endless, rolling water.

a) Name the four Great Lakes that I had the good fortune to gaze upon as the first white man. Find them on a map. Looking carefully at their shape, size and situation, create a legend about their origin — go as far back in time as you can!

b) If the Great Lakes had never existed, how do you think this continent would have evolved? Would many things have changed? What things? In a group, discuss these changes as to the geography, climate, and population of the area.

c) In what other countries can you find lakes that have an influence on the conditions of regions around them? Draw up a list of five of these lakes, and categorize them under the headings: name of country, size of lake, usage of lake (for example, fishing, trade route, or hydroelectric power, which I believe exists in your century).

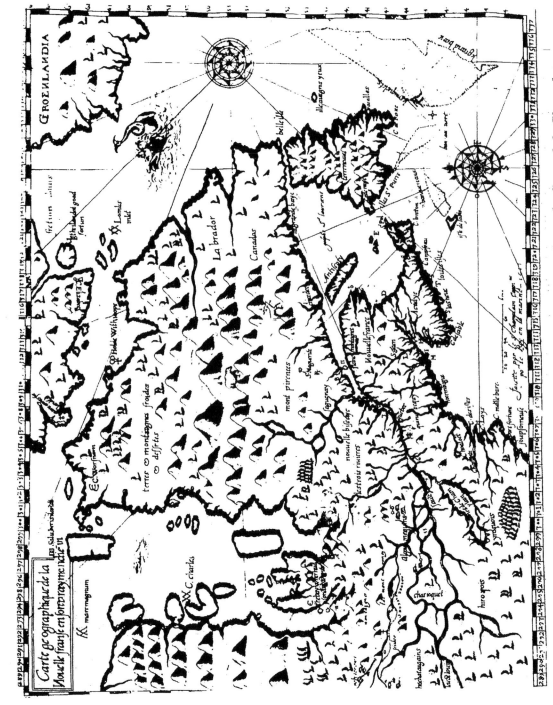

A map of New France drawn by Samuel de Champlain

French Against English

It wasn't the lakes that were the principal attraction for the English in New France. It was the St. Lawrence River — and the fur trade. In 1629, the French in Québec had suffered a particularly bad winter. The English profited from this situation by sinking the French ships that had come with supplies to the colony. With neither defences nor resources, the town of Québec was quickly seized. As for me, I became a prisoner of the English, and as such I had to help pilot their vessels! Some have called me a traitor because of this. It isn't so; I wasn't a traitor! The proof lies in the fact that several people of your century have hailed me as the first Franco-Ontarian. It would greatly please me to think of myself as that.

a) You are the aide-de-camp of Sieur de Champlain in Québec. You are gazing with disbelief at the English vessels coming up the St. Lawrence River. Write a report on your observations in simple and precise language. Don't hesitate to make your feelings, suggestions and hypotheses known to your commander.

b) As for me, Brûlé (or Brusle, as I was called), I found myself on board an English ship. Try to imagine what I would be feeling. Was I then an ignoble traitor, or an unfortunate prisoner? Give your opinion in writing.

c) Create a dialogue between Nicolas Marsolet, my shipboard companion and interpreter of the Montagnais and Algonquian languages, and myself, when we view the cliffs at Québec from the deck of an English vessel. With a friend, produce a little skit based on this scene and present it to the group.

d) Sieur de Champlain is a prisoner in English hands. He blames me most strongly for the situation in which he finds himself. Did I have a choice? Would events have turned out differently if I had acted differently? Prepare a debate on the subject with someone who is not of your opinion. Let the class cast its vote for the winner.

Part of A PALISADED HURON-IROQUOIS VILLAGE

C.W.JEFFERYS

Creek

Entrance Gate

Corn Fields

ALGONKIN CANOE, OLD TYPE.

What Crime Had I Committed?

In 1632, New France was handed over to Governor Champlain. I died the following year under dreadful conditions.

a)   In your opinion, why did the Hurons execute me — because it certainly was an execution — in this horrible way? Had they indeed found me guilty of treachery towards their revered Champlain? Had I tarnished their honour? Had I been a threat to them? Were they trying to strengthen their bond with the French? Think hard about these questions (the historians of your time haven't come up with decisive answers yet), and share your opinion with your friends in a round-table discussion.

b)   If I were living in your time, I would not be an explorer-interpreter as I was in mine. As you know my good points and my bad ones, my strengths and weaknesses, what vocation would *you* think I would choose in your day? Pick at least three that would attract me, given my kind of temperament and personality. Justify your choices; discuss them in a group. I'm waiting impatiently to hear from you.

Goodbye, my friends! I wish you a life full of great and wonderful adventures, like mine. Ah, *la folle aventure!*

Étienne Brûlé

Gabriel Lalemant

Sainte-Marie-des-Hurons,
le vingt-et-unième jour de janvier
de l'an de grâce 1649

Salve, Discipule — Greetings, Student,

　　My name is Gabriel Lalemant. I believe you will learn much from my story. It is going to allow you to enter the world of the Jesuits of the seventeenth century. You are going to accompany me to New France, where my soul was filled with enthusiasm and hope. My great desire was to spread the word of Jesus. His suffering became mine, as my earthly life was dedicated to his service. My faith was present in every aspect of my daily life.

　　May the grace of God go with you!

Le père Gabriel Lalemant, s.j.

Gabriel Lalemant — Atironta

1610-1649

May almighty God bless you, and give you the courage to listen to my story. I greet you, my student. My name is Gabriel Lalemant. I was born in Paris on October 31, 1610. I was the son of a lawyer and the nephew of two Jesuit superiors in Québec. What a heavy heritage to have, don't you think? I bore the name of a distinguished family; I had a keen mind, but very delicate health. It was my soul, impatient as it was to serve God, that directed me to the mission in New France, a mission of life and death for me — my death in the service of the Jesuits. I was scarcely 20 when I joined this religious order in 1630, guided by my faith and devotion.

In 1625, the Jesuits arrived in the land of the *Sauvages,**** under the direction of my uncle Charles Lalemant, their first superior in New France. The "Blackrobes" — the *robes noires* — as we were soon to be called by the Hurons, why did they come to this hard, unforgiving land? Power, riches, prestige, peace? Oh no! It was a deep, religious fervour, a total self-denial that guided their steps. For them, there was nothing in New France to attract the ambitious, the haughty, the lazy or the greedy. There was only work, deprivation, and perhaps death. Like obedient soldiers, they followed the orders of their generals in the Society of Jesus, and they followed them willingly.

"Gabriel, listen to the voice of your conscience. You who are the innocent one, pure, sincere and passionate, what did *you* want to do for the glory of Jesus Christ?"

"You know what I wished more than anything else — to be sent to the other side of the world, to New France, to bring Christianity to the *Sauvages*."

"And what did you do to bring this about?"

"Why are you asking me so many questions?"

"It is my right to question you, to find out your intentions. Without me you would have wandered here and there aimlessly. I was the one who encouraged you to become a thinker, a philosopher, and a theologian. Without me, your death would have been in vain."

"That is true, that is true. How right you are!"

And in truth, in 1632, I added a vow to the other three which I had already taken. I decided to devote myself to a foreign mission; I never stopped praying to God for the order to depart for New France. I shed many tears and sighed many sighs, but I heard no response from Him.

"I know, Gabriel, I know. However, the ways of the Creator are not always clear, God's thoughts are often difficult to interpret. You did not know it then, but you were preparing yourself spiritually for the life you desired."

---

*The French word *Sauvages* was used in a positive sense, meaning "those who lived in freedom, those who were the friends of nature." *Sauvages* has a Latin root, *silva*, meaning a "woodland."

"Yes, I suppose so, but there was nothing to indicate that then."

"Gabriel, you did not give me the opportunity."

Well, I continued my teaching and my studies in France: I was a professor at the college in Moulins, then a student in theology in Bourges. After that, I was minister to the students at the Jesuit College of La Flèche. Then I returned to Bourges as professor of Philosophy, and was in fact prefect of the college for 14 long years. My career was going well.

"Yes, Gabriel. Your mind was developing, your experience was broadening. You were no longer the fervent young man of 1632. The same flame burned within you, but its heat could now be felt from afar."

"Words...all words...I wanted action!"

"Calm yourself, Gabriel. Action was to come your way."

"Yes, finally, in the year of grace 1646, I was chosen for the mission in New France. I departed, ready to devote myself body and soul to the mission. I even drew up a list of my duties to God. Do you want to know what I wrote?"

"Yes, what did you write, Gabriel? I ask you, because after your death your Jesuit brothers found this manuscript and studied it."

"I listed the reasons for my passions."

"These terms are opposites, Gabriel; they are contradictory. What sort of passion has a reason?"

"Well, what do you want me to say, the reasons for my intentions? Anyway, there are seven of them:

To pay back the enormous debt I owe my Saviour, who gave everything, I shall follow his example.

To recognize His grandeur, goodness and glory, I shall serve Him completely.

To pay for the sins which I have committed, I shall undergo enormous suffering.

To show my gratitude towards my family, I shall surrender myself so that they need not blaspheme.

To..."

"Indeed, Gabriel, you had enthusiasm, sincerity and charity. I know that. But what was going to put these qualities to the test once you arrived in Québec? Did you have a strong spirit to go with your admirable devotion?"

"I was a Jesuit. My faith would not falter."

"But your trials were going to prove very difficult, Gabriel."

"Yes, that's true."

I arrived in Québec on September 29, 1646, and stayed there for almost two years. There, it was the harsh winters, the inhospitable land, and the constant danger from the *Sauvages* that actually helped us renew our faith. My two uncles, Charles and Jérôme Lalemant, had preceded me. Uncle Charles was the first Jesuit superior in New France, and a very fine correspondent. Uncle Jérôme, also a Jesuit superior, was the author of the *Jesuit Relations* (the history of the Jesuits in New France) written between 1639 and 1644. (Uncle Charles was going to take on this job in 1651.) Uncle Jérôme wrote the *Journal of the Jesuits*; he created the important institution of the *donnés* (our helpers at the mission who were not ordained — laymen).

"I am pleased to see you were influenced by your family, Gabriel. Now, it was *your* turn. What a burden for your feeble shoulders to bear!"

"If my shoulders were weak, my faith was unshakeable."

"And you certainly needed your faith where you were going — Huronia!"

In September, 1648, I found myself in Huronia, the area between lakes Huron and Ontario. As the Hurons were allies of the French, it was easier for us to win their trust. I would start my work at last.

"And you did it with remarkable zeal, Gabriel, rejecting the spirits, the manitous of the Native peoples — the spirits to be found in the animals, the rivers and the lakes."

"They *wanted* to know our God. They welcomed us with open arms. They even accepted our first permanent settlement in North America at Sainte-Marie-des-Hurons."

"Yes, so I heard. And you learned their language so that you could be nearer to them."

"I studied diligently, drawing on the humility and charity I found in my soul. In February, I was given the mission at Saint-Louis, when Father Chabanel had to leave."

"Your successes were fast in coming, Gabriel, or rather Atironta, as the Hurons called you."

"Yes, everything was going well until that terrible day...that day when...."

"That day when, for the sake of God, you abandoned the honours of your heritage and took up the cross of Jesus."

"Yes...yes...I cannot tell this story. You do it, you know the details."

"So be it. Before dawn on the 16th day of March, 1649, 1,000 Iroquois took the settlement of Saint-Ignace with little difficulty. They made their way to the mission at Saint-Louis — your mission, about three miles* away — and took it at the third attempt. You refused to try to escape. You and Father Brébeuf were both captured. Must I continue, Gabriel?"

"Whatever you wish...whatever you wish..."

"According to the *Jesuit Relations* — from Christophe Regnaut's account — a few Hurons who had escaped the Iroquois were witnesses to the events I describe here. They said that the Iroquois burned all the huts at the mission and then put out their anger on you, Gabriel, and on Father Brébeuf. You were stripped and bound to stakes. A long martyrdom followed. Father Brébeuf died at four o'clock in the afternoon; you Gabriel, with the delicate body and the strong spirit, lasted till nine o'clock the next morning. The mission came for your remains, and buried them under the chapel at Sainte-Marie-des-Hurons on the 21st of March. Later, your remains were venerated in Québec by your uncle Charles Lalemant. Gabriel, are you still there?"

"Yes...yes...God chose me as a sacrifice. I was the last to join the struggle, the first to receive the crown."

---

* As you know, my student, one of our miles is the same as 1.6 km in your time.

The Jesuits

I am going to tell you about the Jesuits. It was Saint Ignatius Loyola, born in 1491 in Azpeitia (in the region now known as Spanish Basque country), who founded the Society of Jesus in Paris in 1534. The *Constitutions* which he drew up for the order were approved by the Pope in 1540. Saint Ignatius, a nobleman, an intellectual and a mystic, left a collection of meditations entitled *Spiritual Exercises*. This collection is still the foundation of the spirituality of our order. My uncles Charles and Jérôme Lalemant are two important Jesuits of the mid-seventeenth century. Other important figures of the time are Paul le Jeune, François le Mercier, Paul Ragueneau and Jean de Brébeuf.

a) According to you, what role did the Jesuits play in the development of New France? What would have happened without them? Were there other people or other associations that could have assumed the same responsibilities? Research in your library so that you can justify your opinion, and prepare a presentation on this subject to read to the class.

b) Find the Jesuit college nearest your home or school. I suggest that you write a letter to its administrators asking them to inform you of the kind of education offered there. This letter must be carefully written as the Jesuits prize education highly.

c) Imagine that you are a young Jesuit training in New France in the mid-seventeenth century. With three friends, write a skit telling of your first encounter with the Native peoples. Think about all the possible aspects of this meeting, and not only of its religious ones. Once the skit is written, stage it, rehearse it and present it to the class.

It is against the background of the "Blackrobes" (as the Hurons called us) that we shall re-enact the special events that were at the centre of my entire life. Accompany me! *Vade mecum....*

Aſſi o domini noſtri Jeſu

Chriſti ſecundum Marcum.

In illo tépore Erat Paſcha et azyma

poſt bídu um. Et ḡ rebant ſummiſacerdotes et ſcrí

be: quomodo Jeſum dolo tenerent et occíderent.

Dicebát autem. S Non in dí e feſto. C Ne forte tu

A Spanish liturgical book by Joannes a Plaça of Toledo, dated 1576, b

a masterpiece of typography and book decoration

1576

Ave Maria — Hail Mary

"Ave Maria!" I know this greeting so well, and I cherish it. It is one of the most important prayers in Catholicism, the Christian religion that recognizes the authority of the pope. The prayer is made up of the traditional words of the Archangel Gabriel and Elizabeth, with additions written in the fifteenth century. The words and feelings the "Ave Marias" express are so beautiful that several versions have become well-known melodies. I listened to or recited many different ones in the course of my life. Their simplicity will never leave me. I love especially the one adapted from a song written in the sixteenth century by Jacob Arcadelt of Holland.

a) Jacob Arcadelt's song is written in Latin. I studied Latin for a long time, as we Jesuits wrote and spoke in that language throughout our training and preaching. It was the language of ancient Rome and its empire. Find out more about the dead languages, and have a discussion about their usefulness in your time. Your group should find many Latin and Greek roots of English words, if you search in a good dictionary.

b) Almost every art form, whether it be music, painting, sculpture or architecture, has a sacred origin: the works have been created to honour a divinity, to sing its praises, or to decorate the places where it is to be venerated. Think about the sacred character of those first works of art, then write an article for a magazine for the arts where you will try to explain this aspect to your readers. The title of your article will be: "The Sacred Roots of Art."

c) Now you will be a composer. Choose a religious or sacred theme that touches or interests you. Write a simple tune and give it to one of your friends as a present.

Ave Maria
by Jac. Arcadelt. (1550.)

Adapted by
FRANK DAMROSCH.

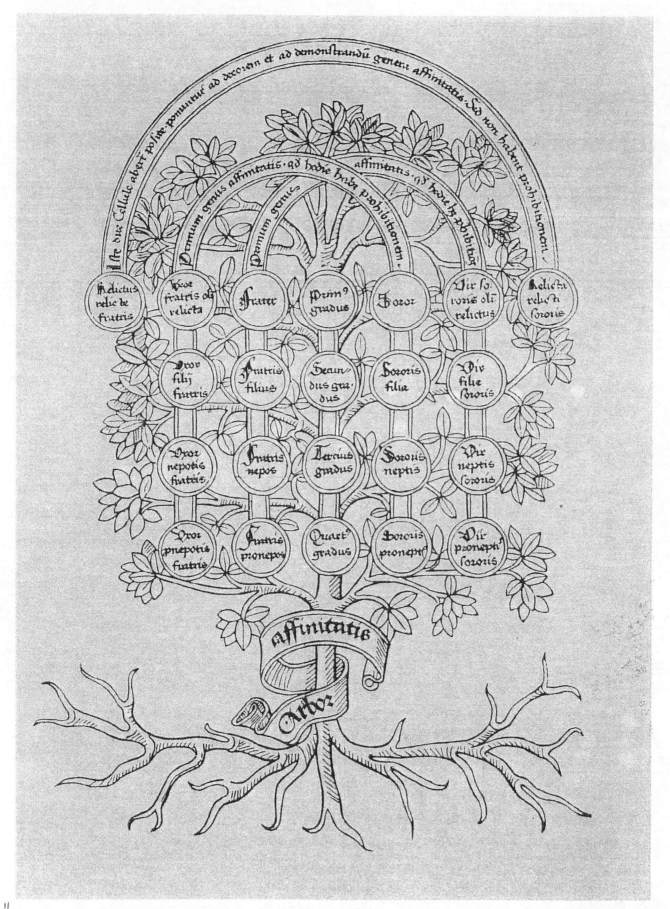

TREE OF AFFINITIES was used in medieval times to determine the relation that a husband and a wife each bears to the kin of the other. The illustration, a woodcut made in 1473 by Johannes Andrei, is reproduced with the permission of the Pierpont Morgan Library.

Our Heritage

Is there by chance a musician perching up there on a branch of your family tree? No? I do not have one either — as far as I know! Among my ancestors there were some wise people — lawmakers and theologians — intellectuals who were expecting me to prove my worth also. I hope I did not disappoint them too much.

a) Make your own family tree. To obtain good results, you must consult the members of your family (write to them, if they live far away and you do not see them very often), and ask questions about your ancestors on both the maternal and paternal sides. Try to find out what country they came from; if possible, ask why they left their native land and came to the country you now call Canada. Also, look for documents (old letters and postcards, birth certificates and citizenship papers) and of course photographs.

b) Your heritage is something passed on from your parents, something you inherit from preceding generations. As the dictionary states, it is "considered as your personal property. You have ownership of that transmitted by your ancestors." Write about what constitutes *your* heritage, in as much as you see it.

c) I know you are young and creative, and I am sure you like to have your imagination take flight on occasion. I would like you to draw a cartoon in which the principal character is the inheritor of something very special. Use precise language to explain what you mean. Your story will be interesting and entertaining, I am sure.

d) What is a hereditary disease? Do some research on this subject, and make a list of hereditary diseases indicating their names, the percentage of people who suffer from them, their respective causes, the chances of cures (treatment), and the research into them carried out in your century. Consult a medical encyclopedia or question your doctor, who will be pleased to help you, I am sure.

At a Catholic mission station 70 miles north of the capital city of Salisbury, a Dominican nun surveys the deceptively serene countryside of Zimbabwe.

The Mission

Physical and mental illness, misfortune and calamity were part and parcel of our religious mission in New France. My dear student, think about all the things that made those missions so risky: an inhospitable land, harsh winters, basic housing and a frugal diet. Add to those the differences of language and customs of the Native peoples. It is in this environment that we, the "Blackrobes," preached. We felt it was our duty to convert the Indigenous peoples; we soon became an important group in the colony. The first French Roman Catholic mission was founded in Tadoussac, a settlement at the mouth of the Saguenay River. There the Jesuits erected a wooden chapel for the Native population and the fur traders — the first chapel built in New France. We also founded schools and convents in Montréal, Québec and Trois-Rivières. We built hospitals for the *Sauvages*, and we built them for the colonists. The mission permitted us an exciting life, but a dangerous one also.

a)   Enquire about the missionary movement in your neighbourhood churches, mosques, synagogues and temples. (Other terms may be used for "missionary movement.") You will be given brochures and flyers that will provide you with accurate facts. Study these carefully with three friends, and use them to make diagrams and graphs. Be precise, showing the world distribution of religious missions, the number of missionaries working in them, and the success of their efforts. Present the results of this enquiry to the whole class, offering your conclusions and predictions for the future of missions in your time.

b)   You are a bishop. Your diocese must send several priests and lay people (those who have taken vows but are not ordained) to a mission abroad. Your administrators and you decide to launch a bold publicity campaign to inform the public of this important project. Put together a committee, and outline the plan of this campaign with the help of illustrations, maps, reports and letters.

The Jesuit Simon Le Moyne with the peacemaker Garakontié of the Onondaga nation, one of the nations of the Iroquois League

The Blackrobes — Les robes noires

It often happens that certain names, nicknames and terms are created to point out an outstanding feature of someone or something. These names may arise from prejudice and ignorance, or they may be there to simplify and clarify the object. In our case, it is easy to guess the origin of the term that was used for us in New France. We Jesuits conformed to the rules of the Society of Jesus in everything including our dress.

a) It is up to you, my student, to give *your* opinion of the style and practicality of our dress. Imagine a long black robe, roomy, with a hood. We have to wear it in all seasons, no matter the weather; we may be travelling by canoe or on horseback. The Native peoples are dressed in a much simpler way of course, but our black robes are all we possess. Think of the advantages and disadvantages of such a garment, and create a different one that might be more suited to the type of life we have to lead. Design it in detail, naming each part and its function. Do not forget that we are in the seventeenth century, in a land of harsh winters and hot summers.

b) Find the nicknames of six famous people in history. Give your opinion of these names, and suggest others that would have been just as appropriate.

c) You are a member of the Society of Jesus. Each month you must write a report on Huronia to the Jesuit superior in Québec. He will put it into the *Jesuit Relations*, published in Paris. You must be precise and concise, respectful and truthful. So, to work, as it conquers all if done with a will. *Labor omnia vincit improbus.**

---

*This Latin proverb comes from a work by Virgil, the Roman poet of 70-19 BC. It is from two lines in his work, the *Georgics*, a poem on farming.

Wallerand Vaillant (1623-1677). Letters with Quill and Penknife, 1658.
(20¼ × 16″) Gemäldegalerie, Dresden.

Charles Lalemant
1587-1674

The proverb I just quoted could have been the motto of my uncle Charles Lalemant, the first Jesuit superior in Québec, from 1625-1629, and missionary from 1634-1638. He was the one who helped Sieur de Champlain in his last illness, and he was the one who officiated at his funeral. He had a solid practicality about him, and showed great kindness towards the French population who loved him in return. He played an important role in the founding of Ville-Marie (Montréal in your day, and indeed in our day before it was called Ville-Marie). He introduced Sieur de Maisonneuve to M. de la Dauversière of the Society of Notre-Dame in Montréal. He was a prodigious correspondent, always writing to his brother Jérôme and to numerous others with whom he maintained a steady flow of letters. What happened to this pile of letters, then? Alas, we do not know.

a) What advantages were there for the Society of Jesus in having such a man as its superior? Write an official letter to the then governor of New France praising my uncle Charles.

b) Imagine the scene at Samuel de Champlain's funeral. You are the reporter who must do the broadcast for the television news that evening (I know this sort of medium exists in your century). Use your imagination, but at the same time remember that you are in New France in the seventeenth century. Prepare your program, rehearse it well and present it to the class.

c) Create a coat of arms which could represent the life of my uncle Charles. You know his qualities and his philosophy; try to incorporate them into the design. Use some Latin if you can; he would like that.

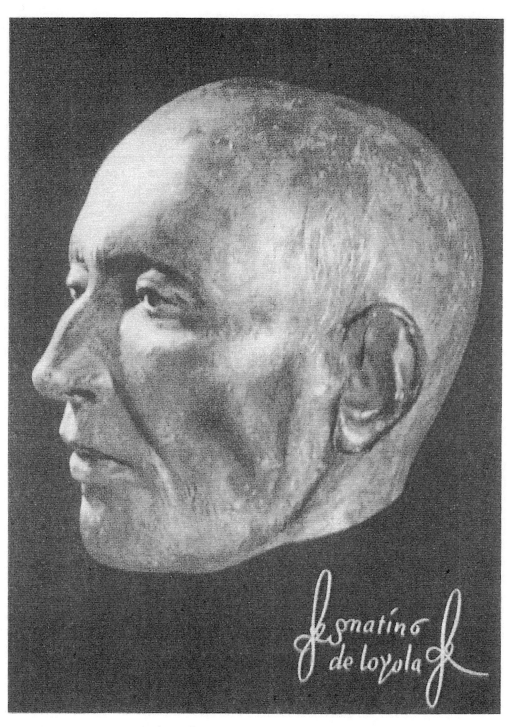

Masque mortuaire de Loyola.
Collection Frère Gebhardt Fröhlich.

Death mask of St. Ignatius Loyola, founder of the Society of Jesus in 1534 in Paris

My Conscience

Deep in my soul, I knew that the qualities and philosophy of my uncle Charles were also a driving force within *me*. This inner voice pushed me, coaxed me, encouraged me and scorned me in turn. It was as if each step I took was being judged by this powerful force — my conscience.

a) My dear student, I beg you to be honest in carrying out the task I am about to set you. Write a page in your diary based on a real-life happening where you were torn between opposing thoughts, when you hesitated between two paths, and did not know which one to take. Looking back, what do you think about the one you chose? Some people say that "just as the fire tests gold, so does misery test strength of character." *Ignis aurum probat, miseria fortes viros.* (Here is another Latin phrase for you.) Could this saying have applied to your choice?

b) With your group, write a skit describing the difficulties a person faces when he/she must make a choice between opposite paths or ways. Express as well as you can the breadth of emotions felt, from frustration to contentment, anger to calm, incredulity to faith. Become actors!

c) "He or she was a person without a conscience." Beginning your first paragraph with this sentence, retell a legend that could have been passed down orally from generation to generation, and that *you* will write down for the very first time.

Last Supper. Seuse, Bourges, 1470.

Jesus Christ

The Bible, this collection of sacred writings divided into two parts — the Old and the New Testaments — is a fine example of stories and prophesies that existed orally long before their written form. We know of the life and work of Jesus Christ through the Gospels. According to our Christian dogma, Jesus is the Son of God and is the Messiah whose coming was announced by the prophets. We have some details about his birth and his youth, and of course his missions in Galilee and Jerusalem. We know also about his death, but we know almost nothing about what he did between the ages of 18 and 30. Some scholars believe that he spent these crucial years travelling, mainly in the East, where he studied the ancient religions. After his death and resurrection, his disciples went far and wide spreading his new religion throughout the then known world.

a) What religions do you know of, other than your own (if you practise one, that is)? Do some research on the topic, make a list of four religions, and classify them under the headings: founder, date of founding, principal doctrines, country, number of followers.

b) Read some stories about the lives of Moses, Jesus, Buddha, or Mohammed. Choose one story that particularly interests you. Read it aloud and present it to the class with a piece of music in the background to create the desired atmosphere. Dim the lights to give a mysterious aura to the whole scene.

c) In a group, prepare a series of *tableaux vivants*, where you and your friends will assume silent, still poses to represent scenes. The subject is the life of Christ or any other founder of a religion. You will need a narrator to tell about the events depicted, along with actors to mime the scenes. Study the themes of your *tableaux vivants* carefully before presentation to ensure their success.

FACSIMILE OF HANDWRITING OF GABRIEL LALEMANT, S.J.

[Selected from his copy of Chevalier de Sillery's donation to the Jesuits, dated Paris, February 22, 1639.]

New France — La Nouvelle-France

New France, my dear student, can be depicted in a series of *tableaux vivants* that show a way of life both rough and extraordinary. As you already know, in the seventeenth century the French possessions in North America were known as New France. Three things come to my mind when I hear this name: religion — mainly the conversion of the Native peoples — the fur trade, and new territory. Although I played the role of a Jesuit missionary in this great drama that was unfolding, I also recognized the importance of the roles played by the merchants, the military, and the coureurs de bois. I did not approve of all the methods they used or all the decisions they took, but I had to admit that without them, New France would not have been such a flourishing colony.

a)   Think about the three themes mentioned above. Write about each one of them, explaining how, together, they made it possible for the colony to survive and grow.

b)   Make a study of my era. Imagine you are the editor-in-chief of a large weekly newspaper. With the help of a founder, president, head of production, journalists and graphic artists, you are about to turn out an edition of the newspaper to be published in Québec, a paper that will describe the New France of the seventeenth century. Create interesting headlines, articles and illustrations, and give your paper a name.

c)   Study the old maps of this area, especially those of Samuel de Champlain. Draw your own. Do not forget the compass points, scale and legend, and pay close attention to detail.

A Dutch sailing vessel of the mid-seventeenth century

Jacob A. Bellevois (1621 - 1676)   Gomshall Gallery, Gomshall-Surrey
Schepen voor de haven van Vlissingen (detail) / Shipping outside Flushing harbour (detail) /
Schiffe vor dem Hafen von Vlissingen (Ausschnitt) / Des bateaux devant le port de Flessengue
(détail) / Barcos fuera del puerto de Flesinga (detalle)

Voyages

The existence of accurate maps makes travelling much easier in your time. Perhaps they take away something of the mystery that shrouded *our* first ocean crossings, something of the feeling of the unknown that filled us at the start of our voyages. Very often we did not know what we were going to find at the end of those voyages, or indeed if we were going to survive them at all. Right from the beginning, from the times of Jacques Cartier and Samuel de Champlain, the newly arrived colonists had found this land cold and desolate. Few of them had survived these first harsh years. The hardships of the long voyage had weakened some and killed others, even before they had reached *terra firma*. Once the survivors had set foot on land, they committed themselves body and soul to a rough pioneer life, and to the never-ending cycle that is the struggle to survive.

a)   Do some research on the large sailing vessels that set off into the oceans in the seventeenth century. Draw one in detail with its masts, different types of sails and flag. Find a picture of a large, modern ocean liner. Compare the two types of ships.

b)   Well before Jacques Cartier and Samuel de Champlain, there were many, many seafarers who took to the oceans with a bold spirit, in search of unknown lands. They travelled hundreds of miles before reaching port safely — and sometimes they did not manage *that*. There were the Phoenicians, the Celts and the Vikings, for example. Do some research on the exploits of a few of these peoples, and create a mini-project with maps, drawings and pictures. (Do not forget to show the ocean currents, and the passages or channels the boats could pass through.) Write a brief account of the seafaring people you have mentioned, giving the names of the countries "discovered", the dates of the voyages, the oceans crossed, and the aim of the odyssey.

c)   Make up a list of the great explorers of the fifteenth, sixteenth and seventeenth centuries using the following headings: name, nationality, date of voyage, port of departure, areas explored.

d)   Has someone you know, or have you yourself taken a journey which has completely changed your life? Prepare an account of it and present it orally to your group. It is said that just as we influence our times, so do our times influence us. *Tempora mutantur nos, et mutamur in illis.*

Il naquit à Paris le 3me d'octobre de l'année 1610. Il entra en notre compagnie, le 24me de mars de l'année 1630. Il y est mort dans un lit de gloire le 17me de mars de la présente année 1649. Les Hurons le nommaient Atironta.

Ego infrascriptus superior missionis Canadensis, societatis Jesu, juratus affirmo me supradicta de morte Patris Joannis de Brebeuf et Patris Gabrielis Lallemant, a testibus oculatis et fide dignis, accepisse, meque ipsum multarum rerum fuisse oculatum testem. Datum Kebeci, in Nova francia, die decima quarta Decembris 1652.

Paulus Ragueneau, s. j.

A French and Latin text from the Jesuit Relations referring to Father Jean de Brébeuf and Father Gabriel Lalemant, written by Paul Ragueneau

Figures of Speech

Eloquence — the skill of being able to speak well, and the capability of being able to inspire in a positive way — is a very desirable quality. An oral presentation in which no attention has been given either to diction or style will have less effect on your listeners than a text where both the form and the content have been considered. The Latin language was quite natural for us, priests, teachers and students. Of course we were not all capable of reaching the heights of a Cicero, the famous Roman orator and writer who lived from 106-43 BC. However, the advantages of speaking clearly and assertively were always evident to us.

a) My dear student, you heard these words in my opening story: "The same flame burned inside you, but its heat was now felt from afar." What does this sentence mean? Comment on the image used here, suggesting other images or metaphors that could be used to express a similar idea.

b) The use of figures of speech such as simile, metaphor, contrast, onomatopœia and alliteration, aims to move and impress the listener. Make a list of these figures of speech and look up their definitions. Give two examples of each one in writing (you can find examples in specialized books). Finally, make up your own examples, one for each figure of speech. How about the word "Blackrobes," the name the Hurons called us — what figure of speech is that?

c) You are a poet who likes to write beautiful, clear verses. Choose a theme from New France that really interests you. Think about it, and let it touch your emotions: you will probably feel many different emotions. Let the words come (with a little patience and a lot of work). Read the poem aloud, practise it and record it choosing special music as a background. Have a friend or group listen to it.

The Huron carol, written by Father Jean de Brébeuf

Prayer

In a prayer, we address the Creator (his or her name will vary depending on our religion). Sometimes the prayer takes the form of a poem or song. I am sure you have heard many prayers; I know *I* have, as my Jesuit education filled me with them — whispered, murmured, recited, chanted, sung and even shouted. My soul overflowed with supplications, invocations, litanies, orations....

I remember in particular a Christmas carol composed by Father Jean de Brébeuf, my superior in the Jesuit order. He had written it in the Huron language so that the Huron people could sing it. (They were his faithful followers, his "flock" as we often said.) You will find this hymn to be quite different from the other prayers and carols we sang in our churches. I am sure you know the reason why.

a)   Try to find a recording of the Huron carol. Listen to it and practise it in a group, then sing it to the class.

b)   Look in the Bible or any other religious work — the Koran, for example — and see if you can find prayers written for different reasons. You will see that many of them have to do with everyday life. Choose one you like particularly, and write a simplified version of it.

c)   Each religion has its rites and ceremonies that allow its followers to express their beliefs publicly, and pass them on to future generations. In this way, spiritual realities become physical gestures and oral texts. Let each member of your group choose a religion that he or she will study for its beliefs, rites and ceremonies, doctrines, and influence on the believer. Have a round-table discussion about your findings.

d)   I would like you to find pictures of people at prayer in an art book or museum, for example. Do some research on four of these people, and as the director of a museum, write a paragraph on each one with the aim of inserting the text into the museum catalogue or guidebook.

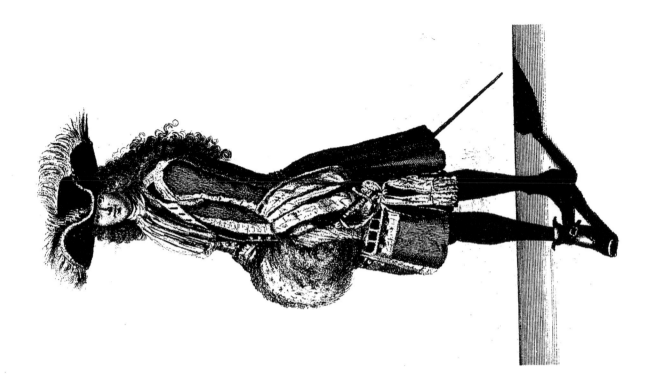

French male costume, 1693

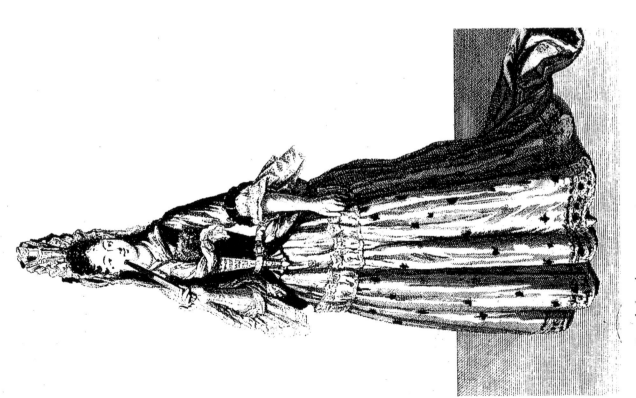

French female costume, 1693

Québec[*]

Come, let me be your guide along the snow-covered routes of Québec. Oh, the harshness of the winters! As you know, I spent two years in Québec, this fortified town founded by Sieur de Champlain in 1608. It was not like any of the French towns I had known. Québec is built on an escarpment overlooking the St. Lawrence River where the St. Charles River flows into it. Québec's ramparts stand atop steep cliffs — almost perpendicular to the water, and very difficult to scale. It was here in Québec that the political administrators and the heads of religion resided: the governor and his family at the governor's mansion — afterwards Fort Saint-Louis — the rich people in the Upper Town, the townsfolk along the river in the Lower Town. I learned that later on, the style of the rich became quite fine and elegant in this pretty little town, the hub of our colony. As for the ordinary workers, many spent their days in unhealthy and dangerous conditions (there was among other things a great risk of fire). Warehouses near the port basins where many worked were steadily filling with furs; the colony as a whole was becoming more and more prosperous.

a)   With three friends, take on the roles of Samuel de Champlain and his aides. After you have informed yourself about his voyages to New France, write a dialogue in which the choice of the site for Québec is discussed. Each person will contribute to the discussion in as meaningful a way as possible. Present the scene to the whole class.

b)   Imagine you are a young lay person residing in Québec about the middle of the seventeenth century; maybe you are part of the governor's entourage, or perhaps you are in charge of an important warehouse situated down by the river. You keep a journal in which you write a weekly account of what has happened. Be honest with yourself, and think of all the aspects of your daily life in Québec: your workday business affairs of course, but also your private life.

c)   I have heard that a large town now exists on the site of Québec. Do you know this place? Draw up a list of the advantages and disadvantages of living in this town in your century rather than in mine.

---

[*] The word *Québec* comes from the *kebec*, the name the Native peoples of the area gave to this place where the river narrowed. Sieur de Champlain liked the name. To Jacques Cartier the place had been the Iroquoian village of Stadacona, 70 years earlier.

Sainte~Marie~au~pays~des~Hurons

SAINTE-MARIE-AU-PAYS-DES-HURONS
1639-1649

Jérôme Lalemant-Achiendassé
1593 - 1673

Like his brother Charles before him, my uncle Jérôme was a superior of the Jesuits in New France. He was at our head from 1645-1650 and from 1659-1665. What filled me most with admiration for him was his work as superior at the Huron mission. He had been named to this position in 1638, the same year he had arrived in New France. His first administrative act was to take a census of the population of Huronia: there were about 12,000 people in the area. In 1639, he began the construction of Sainte-Marie-aux-Hurons (also called Sainte-Marie-des-Hurons), which was going to be the main residence of the missionaries and the most developed outpost in the area.

It was my uncle Jérôme who introduced the institution of the *donnés*, lay helpers who gave themselves over to mission life without taking vows, and who, if necessary, could bear arms. These *donnés* were essential to the survival of the mission, by their numbers alone; in 1649, there were 22 of them in Huronia. There were 16 priests and four assistant brothers (the latter being assigned to domestic chores).

During my uncle's first period as superior of the Jesuits in Québec, from 1645-1650, there were seven martyrdoms in the colony, including Father Jean de Brébeuf's and mine. My uncle returned to France and stayed there for the next few years. In 1659, he came back to Québec and took up the same post, at the express demand of Monseigneur de Laval, Bishop of New France.

a) You can see that I hold my uncle in very high esteem. Is there a historical or contemporary person whom you hold in similar esteem? Write a paragraph describing the person, and another one justifying your choice.

b) According to Father Simon Le Moyne, the name Achiendassé, which the Hurons gave to my uncle, was destined to become the name of all Jesuit superiors in Québec. Think of some names of people or even widely used products that have become generic terms. Machiavelli is one example. He was an Italian politician and philosopher in early sixteenth century Florence. In your day, you use his name in its adjectival form (Machiavellian) to describe a statesperson without scruples, one who wants to attain a political end without caring if the means are just. In a group, draw up a list of generic terms and explain their meaning in writing.

c) In Huronia at this time there were three types of people serving the mission: the Jesuit, the lay brother and the *donné*. The first preached, the second did manual work, and the third helped the others, with or without arms. Form groups of four, in which an interviewer questions each of these people. Present the results of these interviews to the whole class.

RELATION
DE CE
QVI S'EST PASSE'

en la Miſſion des Peres de la Compagnie de IESVS aux Hurons, pays de la Nouuelle France, és années 1648. & 1649.

Enuoyée

AV R. P. HIEROSME LALEMANT, Superieur des Miſſions de la Compagnie de IESVS, en la Nouuelle France.

Par le P. PAVL RAGVENEAV, de la meſme Compagnie.

Pour la faire tenir au R. P. Prouincial de la meſme Compagnie.

A PARIS,

Chez { SEBASTIEN CRAMOISY, Imprimeur ordinaire du Roy, & de la Reyne Regente, ET GABRIEL CRAMOISY, } ruë ſainct Iacques, aux Cicognes.

M. DC. L.

AVEC PRIVILEGE DV ROY.

The Jesuit Relations

The *Jesuit Relations* contain accounts, texts, reports and stories concerning the Jesuit mission in New France in the mid-seventeenth century. They comprise many volumes; they were published in Paris, France, by Sébastien and Gabriel Cramoisy. As I told you in my opening story, my uncles Charles and Jérôme Lalemant contributed greatly to these books. They, along with other Jesuits, wrote detailed accounts of their daily lives in New France. The *Jesuit Relations*, an excellent historical document, was succeeded by the *Journal of the Jesuits*, which has preserved the social, political and religious life of my time for everyone to read.

a) Historians can learn many facts about my time, thanks to written information. Think what they could deduce from examining objects. Imagine that you and I are going to choose five objects that could possibly represent my life in New France. We shall then bury the objects carefully, and wait for their disclosure in your century. Write their descriptions, indicate the reasons for your choice, and draw each one with care.

b) The *Jesuit Relations* are written in French, in an old form of the language, with some additions in Latin, for example: "*In Nova Francia, die decima quarta Decembris, 1648 datum Kebeci.*" (In New France, the 14th day of December, 1648, dated in Québec.) As for the Huron language, the Huron dictionary was written by us with the help of interpreters. Imagine that a Huron chief is recounting his impressions of the coming of the Jesuits into his country. Write his story and read it to the rest of your group.

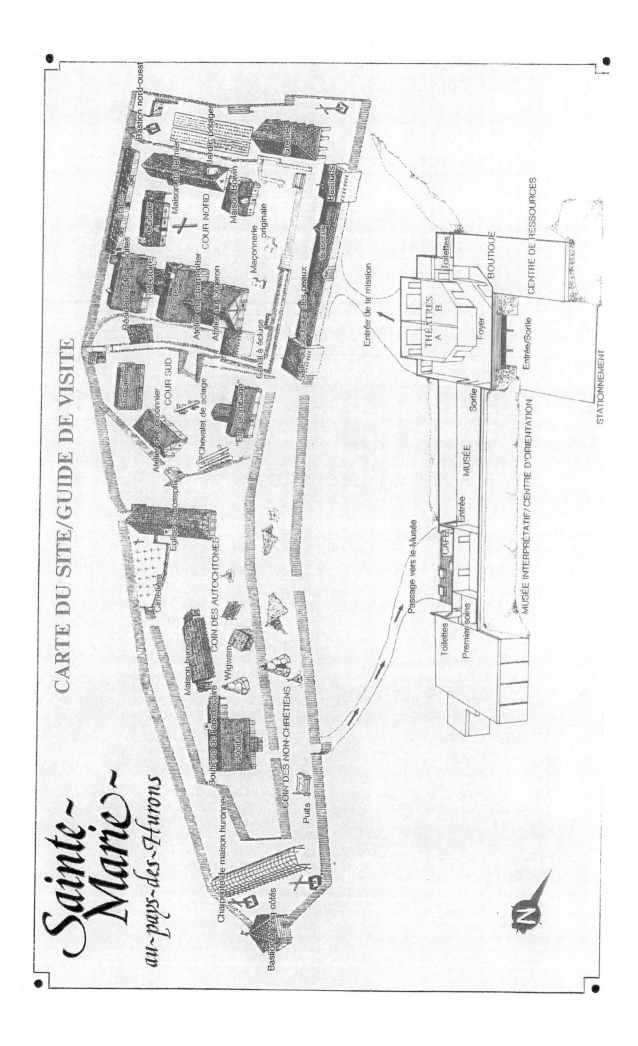

Sainte-Marie-des-Hurons[*]

Before my uncle Jérôme's arrival, there had been no permanent residence for the Jesuits in Huronia. In 1639, my uncle, with the help of Father Jean de Brébeuf and other priests and lay people, decided to build general quarters for the mission. It is in this way that they began the construction of Fort Sainte-Marie. The fortified buildings comprised two chapels, one for the priests and the other for the Hurons, a forge, a woodworking shop, a shoemaker's and a baker's. There was a hospital and a dormitory for the 50 or so *Français* who lived there. In the 1640s, the Iroquois belonging to the League of the Five Nations — Mohawk, Seneca, Oneida, Cayuga and Onondaga — were fighting the other Iroquois bands, namely the Huron, Neutral, Petun and Erie. It was during an attack that the *Français* and the Hurons set fire to their own fort, so that it would not fall into enemy hands. Unfortunately, Sainte-Marie-des-Hurons (also called Sainte-Marie-aux-Hurons, and often in your time Sainte-Marie-au-pays-des-Hurons) had lasted only 10 years before it was burnt to the ground.

a)   If you had been placed in a similar situation, would you have made the same decision, to set fire to the fort? Justify your answer in a paragraph given over to this sorrowful event.

b)   Try to organize a visit to Sainte-Marie-au-pays-des-Hurons. To prepare yourself for the trip to this extraordinary place, find out all you can about it in your local public library. Make a mini-project out of this information, working in a small group, drawing maps, sketches and illustrations. Do not forget to include a short history of the place, as well as possible explanations for the main happenings that took place there. I shall read all this with the greatest of interest.

c)   Create a series of postage stamps depicting the life of the Jesuits, lay brother, *donnés* and Hurons at Sainte-Marie-des-Hurons, between the years 1639 and 1649. Send your finished product to Canada Post with a covering letter. (I believe that is the name of the service.)

The address of this interesting place is: Sainte-Marie-au-pays-des-Hurons; Huronia Historic Park, P.O. Box 160, Midland, Ontario L4R 4K8 telephone: (705) 526-7838

Father Jean de Brébeuf, 1593-1649

Father Jean de Brébeuf
1593-1649

Just as postage stamps can represent the various aspects of life in a country, so can Father Jean de Brébeuf symbolize the faith, trials and misfortunes of the Jesuits in New France. Father Brébeuf came to New France in 1625 with my uncle Charles, Father Massé and two lay brothers. He was the first of us to meet the Native peoples when he reached Lake Huron, in 1634, after a month-long journey from Québec. Father Jean de Brébeuf was appointed superior of the Huron mission, a position my uncle Jérôme took up in 1638. I shared the mission at Saint-Louis — three miles* from the settlement of Saint-Ignace — with Father Brébeuf 11 years later. It was there that we met our fate.

a) Learn about Father Jean de Brébeuf. Write a report explaining what his life and his death could have represented to the Jesuits.

b) We were not the only martyrs at this dreadful time. There were also Antoine Daniel, Charles Garnier, Isaac Jogues, Jean de Lalande, Noël Chabanel, and René Goupil: all beatified by the Church in 1930, as were Father Brébeuf and myself. In the Catholic religion, we eight French Jesuit missionaries who died a violent death in New France from 1642-1649 are known as the *Saints Martyrs du Canada*. Our Saints' day is the 19th of October. Do you know of any other martyrs — belonging to different religions or civilizations — who died for their special causes? Name three, and state their religion or beliefs, the reasons for their martyrdoms, the dates of their lives, and the consequences of the events. We shall ask God's everlasting light to shine on them as it does on others throughout eternity. *Lux aeterna luceat eis, Domine, cum sanctis tuis in aeternum!*

c) In a group, try to justify the presence of the Jesuits in New France. A debate in which four participants — two in favour of their presence, two against — can express their views may follow the discussion.

---

* As you know, my student, one of our miles is the same as 1.6 km in your time.

This is a reproduction of the lead plaque found in the grave of Father Jean de Brébeuf at Fort Sainte-Marie on August 17, 1954.

The Account of Christophe Regnaut

We took our religion to the Native peoples. They had had their own religions for hundreds of years, so it was only natural that there would have been trouble between us. The Iroquois were against our presence in their territory. Christophe Regnaut's report of our martyrdom at their hands occurs in the fourteenth volume of the *Jesuit Relations* written for the year 1649. He writes with great precision, and he ends with these realistic words:

It is not a doctor from the Sorbonne[*] who has written this, you see. It is someone who has been with the Iroquois, someone who has lived through more than he thought he would, who is and always will be,
Sir,
Your most humble and obedient servant,
   Christophe Regnaut

(Ce n'est pas un Docteur de Sorbonne qui a composé cecy vous le voyez bien; c'est un reste d'Iroquois et une personne qui a vescu plus qu'il ne pensoit, qui est et sera toujours,
  Monsieur,
  Votre Tres Humble et tres obéissant serviteur,
  Christophe Regnaut.)

a)   Give an explanation of this conclusion in writing.
b)   We have just read the end of Regnaut's account. This is its title:
"The True Account of the Martyrdom and Blessed Death of Father Jean de Brebœuf and Father Gabriel L'Alemant in New France, in Huron Country by the Iroquois."
Think about these words. In a group, discuss this title and justify the choice of words by the author. If you are opposed to them, state your reasons clearly.

---

[*] The Sorbonne, founded in Paris by Robert de Sorbon, had been a school of Theology since 1257. It had been hostile towards us, the Jesuits, in the sixteenth century. Nowadays, it is a university of great renown.

c) You are going to question one of the editors of the *Jesuit Relations* (the history of the Jesuits in New France) for a radio program. (They tell me that radio is a marvellous invention whereby hundreds of people can listen to something at the same time.) Ask him or her precise questions, and try to elicit good responses. One of your friends can play the role of editor, and you can present the interview to the whole class. I shall be one of your most attentive listeners.

Vade in pace!

Gabriel Lalemant

Marguerite Bourgeoys

Ville-Marie,
le 30 novembre 1663

My dear Student,

My name is Marguerite Bourgeoys. I hope my story is going to please you. You are going to get to know the different feelings of the inhabitants of New France, as each day brings joy and sadness, fear and boldness, anger and pity. I shall introduce you to my good friends, Sieur de Maisonneuve and Jeanne Mance. You will feel for yourself the strength and well-being with which our religion filled our souls.

May the grace of our Holy Mother accompany you always.

Marguerite Bourgeoys

Marguerite Bourgeoys
1620 - 1700

Ah, Troyes! Troyes! It was a pretty little town situated in Champagne, that warm and welcoming region in the northeast of France. But I am dreaming: I am letting myself get carried away. I always did have a creative imagination. *Bonjour*, my dear student! Would you like to accompany me to my home town of Troyes to experience the sights and sounds of the seventeenth century?

My name is Marguerite Bourgeoys. I am a woman of the seventeenth century, greatly influenced by her time and place: influenced by the Thirty Years War, and by the mystics from France and Spain.

"What are you saying, my dear Sister Marguerite? You are a woman of any century!"

"Ah, so it is you, my dear Paul de Chomedey de Maisonneuve! What a pleasure to hear your voice again, my good friend who is so just and humble. I am trying to paint my portrait in words for my readers of the twenty-first century. All *I* was really was the humble servant of the Holy Mother, nothing more, trying hard to fulfil the tasks She gave me."

"And you were admirable in that regard, Sister Marguerite, always innovative in your teaching, and capable of caring for the body as well as the soul. But pass me my lute, my beloved musical instrument, and I shall make music quietly as you continue your story."

I was born on April 17, 1620, the sixth in a family of twelve children. My relations belonged to the French bourgoisie. My father was master candle-maker and coiner at the Mint in Troyes. My mother was a Garnier, people of means also. My childhood was a happy one, nothing out of the ordinary. I was the most joyful of little girls, singing, playing and working with pleasure and good humour. Everyone loved little Marguerite, so carefree and thoughtful."

The years passed. My mother, my sisters Anne and Jeanne, and my brothers Thomas and Nicolas died one by one of the illnesses of the time. As for me, I bounced back from these misfortunes and recovered my joyfulness and my little coquettish ways, not knowing that this carefree state of mind was not going to last for long.

The year was 1640. I was 20 years of age. One beautiful morning in Troyes, I was participating in the procession dedicated to the Companions of the Rosary. I was surrounded by my friends. The ceremony was proceeding normally as we reached the church portal where a beautiful statue of the Madonna stood above the arch. I looked at her and recited my Ave Maria to her; She was so lovely, so serene. Just then I experienced a strange feeling, and became completely overwhelmed. From that moment, I abandoned all these little ways that had been so important to me, and I withdrew from the life I had known to dedicate myself to the service of God. I had been touched by the everlasting grace of God. From then on, I would follow the way of the Holy Mother.

The first stage in my new life took place in the convent of the *congrégantines*, religious women who never went out into the world. They took charge of the education of girls. What interested *me* was that they had founded another congregation that worked out in the community. This group, made up of young laywomen who were of course not cloistered, got together to pray and to learn how to teach. I enjoyed that. I joined this community with enthusiasm, helping the less fortunate and taking vows of poverty, charity and chastity. In all my actions I tried to follow the Holy Mother, She who was not cloistered. I was out in the world, spreading good where it was most needed, without a veil, without a wimple. I was happy in my task.

"And so it was, my good Sister Marguerite, that I met you several years later. That was fortunate for us in New France."

"Ah, yes, my dear Maisonneuve, I was 23 when you came to Troyes to visit your sister, the Reverend Mother Louise de Chomedey de Sainte-Marie, the head of our community. I remember how happy I felt when you accepted my offer to go to New France, that land that drew me to it. Once more, God had shown me the way."

"Neither the stories of the Iroquois attacks nor the unhealthy conditions in the colony could discourage you. I recognized that we had in you a person of exceptional character, when I saw your determination, humility, courage and desire to commit yourself to the service of the less fortunate souls among us."

The year is 1655. Hoist the sails! We are off to New France, to Ville-Marie, that small, fortified village and missionary outpost. It had been founded by Jérôme le Royer de la Dauversière, of the Society of *Notre-Dame de Montréal.*

"Sister Marguerite, you are forgetting me, Marie Dumesnil, who made that crossing with you. I was only 12 and an orphan in my own land when I was entrusted to you by Sieur de Maisonneuve. How I adored you, Sister! You were more than a mother to me, especially at the time of my marriage one year later."

"Marie Dumesnil, yet another voice from the past. Do you remember that crossing of eight weeks — eight long weeks in that dark and grimy little ship tossed about on the sea — then the journey by canoe from Québec to Ville-Marie? At last we met Jeanne Mance, who was to become my dear and fine companion."

"Here *I* am also, dear Sister Marguerite! It is Jeanne Mance here. On the morning you arrived, I told you the sad news that you had no students: all our little ones had died at an early age because of the dreadful conditions in the colony. But, as was your wont, you accepted things as they were. What inner strength you had, Sister Marguerite! Just as *you* never disappointed anyone, you yourself did not stay disappointed for long! You gave yourself completely to the work of the colony. Just like me in my hospital, you were first and foremost a true social worker. With exemplary patience you awaited the day when you could at last practise your profession of teaching."

"And that was not long in coming, my dear Jeanne. It is Maisonneuve here. In 1658 I gave our dear Marguerite a stable — a stable 36 by 18 feet* — made of stone, near your hospital of Saint-Joseph, the Hôtel-Dieu. It was there, in this lowly building, that she began her school for girls — with the young survivors of Ville-Marie."

"Ah, yes, my dear Maisonneuve, how happy I was! I taught my students to read and write, and to perform household duties that would come in useful later on. During the first years, the school ran from spring to autumn and was closed in the winter because of the cold and the snow-

---

* As you know, one of our linear feet is the same as .35 m in your day.

covered routes. I tried to direct and manage my teachers and students just as I had been taught myself in Troyes, giving a solid education to all our children, not only to the daughters of the rich. I demanded patience, devotion and competence from my fellow-workers. It was a fine little stable and a good little school. If the children could not come to us, we went to them, on foot, by canoe, on horseback, by way of river and forest. We were made welcome everywhere we went — right, Jeanne?"

"That is true, Sister Marguerite! You were easily recognized in your dark dress and white fichu and head covering made from Rouen linen. I have to say that *my* dress had more finery than yours! I shall never forget the journey we made to France together in the year of grace 1658. I was so ill, my right arm was hurting so badly that I had to go to Paris to find a cure. But what I found was more of a true miracle, thanks to the reliquary of Jean-Jacques Olier, the mystic. What a wondrous feeling, when I felt the heat fill my body and soul: I was cured! Then there was the return journey with your young ladies and Father le Maistre, the nurses' confessor (who was to die two years later at the hands of the Iroquois). Oh, that most dreadful of journeys, two months in a furious sea being tossed hither and yon, and illness on board. The soldiers, the recruits for the colony, looked on you as an angel, you know, Sister Marguerite."

"Jeanne, I am not worthy of all these compliments. It suffices to say that we both come from the beautiful province of Champagne."

"And so do I, Paul de Chomedey de Maisonneuve. I remember your second journey to France, in 1670, after Monseigneur François de Laval's visit. He was the powerful bishop of New France, and as such he gave his approval of your teaching. You even went to Paris to see King Louis XIV, with 10 sols* in your pocket, with no fine dress to wear, no fine friends to greet you, a woman travelling on her own in those troubled times. It is barely believable! What courage, what perseverance! Messieurs Talon and Colbert had already written a report in your favour. His Majesty gave you the patent letters for teaching you had asked for.

"In the years that followed, you put every effort into realizing your plans, my dear Sister. You founded a boarding school at Ville-Marie, a charity workshop at Pointe Saint-Charles — the first domestic school in our country, in truth — and also schools at Champlain, Point-aux-Trembles and Batiscan. Oh how you worked, joyfully and strongly, Sister Marguerite, welcoming into your schools the less fortunate girls, teaching the Native girls, establishing a mission in the Native village of la Montagne!

"Time went by. I was recalled to France after 23 years of service in Ville-Marie. I was expecting that decision: as you know, I had had my difficulties with the administration. From that day, my day of departure for France, I abandoned my music and did not touch my beloved lute again. My heart was filled with sadness."

"Ours also, my dear, fine friend, but we carried on with our work. The filles du Roi — the daughters of the King — these young women whom Louis XIV sent to New France to start families, continued to arrive. In the space of 10 years, more than 800 of them came to the colony

---

* The sol, one of our coins, was made of either copper or silver, and was usually worth $\frac{1}{20}$ of a livre; a livre, my dear student, was worth a pound of silver.

from our mother country, France. No doubt that was better than the state of affairs in 1666, the year of M. Talon's first census, when there were 719 bachelors counted for 45 young women!"

"Yes, I well remember, Sister Marguerite. You started the first marriage agency in the land with those filles du Roi. You educated and counselled each one who disembarked, and you questioned each man who came in search of a good companion. You had so much tact and sensitivity!"

"Oh, Jeanne, I learned these ways from you. And Jeanne...your death, in 1673...what a huge loss for me! Four years later, the stone chapel of Bonsecours was finished, and in 1680 I went to France on my last visit. In 1693, I handed in my resignation for the second time, still fighting those people who wanted to join us to the Ursuline order. They wanted to make us a cloistered order. But we had to stay out in the world if we wanted to fulfill our mission!"

My physical life came to an end in the year 1700. I wished for *my* death rather than have one of our young and ailing sisters die, Marie Dumesnil's daughter. I had prayed to God to take my life rather than this poor child's. Once again, he heard me.

(Marguerite Bourgeoys was beatified in 1950 and canonized in 1982. The survival of her order [the order of the Congregation of Notre-Dame] proves that her form of mysticism was always accompanied by a firm sense of reality.)

MARGUERITE BOURGEOYS
The sick man walked.

Religion

From the age of 20, and for the rest of my days, I felt that I was guided by the Holy Mother in everything I did. Religion played a fundamental role in my life. The Holy Mother, *Sainte-Marie*, gave birth to Jesus after the Archangel Gabriel had told her about the coming of her Son. Her Son was to be the Messiah. She herself appears several times in the public life of Christ, and her cult spread throughout the West from the beginning of the fourth century. The Church gave her the title of Mother of God, and defined the dogmas of the Immaculate Conception and the Assumption.

a) Do you know of other people who have been equally inspired by their religion, be it Christianity, Judaism, Islam, Hinduism or Buddhism? Write a paragraph about each of them and illustrate your text with diverse pictures (reproductions of engravings, postcards for example).

b) What do you think about this statement: It is thanks to the religious orders that New France flourished as it did? Prepare a presentation on this subject and present it to the class. Expect people to ask questions and also raise objections about what you might say.

c) Religion is defined sometimes as the "cult of the divinity." What is *your* definition, editor-in-chief? Write what you think of the religions of your time for the local weekly or daily paper which you edit. Try to convince your readers. The gift of persuasion is a rare and precious talent.

As you know, religion has been my guiding light through life. It has inspired me in all my actions, aims and desires. Do not think that this constant preoccupation has restrained the passion I have for life! The very opposite, my dear student, my life has been profoundly changed by it — embellished and enriched by it. That is what we are going to see as we try to experience the different feelings that could have enlivened and emboldened me, a religious thinker, teacher, housekeeper, mother of orphans, traveller, pioneer, and sincere friend — for I was *all* of those! Accompany me on this marvellous journey.

Vous êtes à TROYES, Capitale historique de la Champagne.

La richesse du patrimoine mérite un long séjour pour découvrir tous ses trésors.

Nous vous proposons en 1h 30 environ de découvrir en flânant, les sites les plus remarquables en empruntant au départ de l'Eglise St-Jean, le circuit figurant sur ce document. Vous pourrez choisir de rester pour compléter votre visite. Sinon, vous aurez ainsi préparé votre retour dans notre Cité.

L'Office de Tourisme vous propose toute l'année des visites guidées de la Ville par des guides conférenciers. Pour tout renseignement, adressez-vous à l'Office de Tourisme

Welcome to Troyes, the ancient capital of the Champagne region.

You will find it worth your while to spend a few days here, to discover all the town has to offer. We especially recommend that you visit the most interesting areas of the town centre on foot. This will take you about one-and-a-half hours. The itinerary is shown on this leaflet, and the starting point is St John's Church (Eglise St Jean). Afterwards, you may choose to stay a little longer, in order to get to know the town better, or, if not, we feel certain you will want to come back again.

The Tourist Office organizes guided visits of the town all the year round. For further information, contact the Tourist Office

Troyes

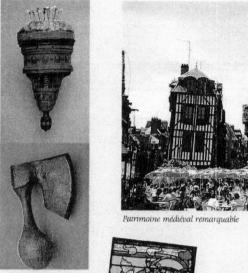

Patrimoine médiéval remarquable

Maison de l'outil : musée unique au monde (10 000 outils anciens)

"Ville Sainte du Vitrail" le plus remarquable ensemble de vitraux en Europe

Spectacles nocturnes dans des édifices prestigieux

Rare jubé sculpté du 16e siècle

Troyes

Sie befinden sich in Troyes. Historische Hauptstadt der Champagne.

Lassen Sie sich Zeit, um unser reiches Kulturgut zu entdecken.
Wir empfehlen Ihnen einen anderthalbstündigen Stadtbummel, der Sie zu den wichtigsten Sehenswürdigkeiten führt. Treffpunkt ist vor der Kirche "St. Jean", der genaue Rundgang wird Ihnen umstehend beschrieben. Sie können auch einen längeren Aufenthalt wählen, um Ihren Stadtbesuch zu vertiefen. Ansonsten lassen Sie sich dazu überreden, ein anderes Mal wiederzukommen.

Das Verkehrsamt bietet Ihnen das ganze Jahr über Stadtführungen, in denen Sie von diplomierten Fremdenführerinnen geleitet werden, an.Für alle weiteren Auskünfte wenden Sie sich an den Verkehrsamt

Ecole Troyenne de sculpture du 16ème siècle

Visites commentées du Vieux Troyes, des Musées, ou circuits-découvertes des environs, avec les Guides-Conférenciers de l'Office du Tourisme, agréés par la Caisse Nationale des Monuments Historiques.

Toutes l'année sur rendez-vous : pour les groupes ou les individuels.

Flâneries d'été dans le Vieux Troyes : de juillet à septembre, visites guidées tous les jours, même dimanche à heure fixes.

Accueil dans les églises : se renseigner à l'Office de Tourisme pour les horaires d'ouverture.

Musée d'Art Moderne : collection exceptionnelle

Welkom in Troyes, historische hoofdstad van Champagne.

Met behulp van de op deze gids aangegeven route met als beginpunt de kerk van St. Jean, nodigen wij U uit om tijdens gedurende een ongeveer 1.30 uur durende wandeling de verschillende bezienswaardigheden van onze stad te ontdekken.
U kunt natuurlijk ook langer blijven om zodoende uw bezoek te kompletteren of aan het einde van de rondleiding direct naar het centrum terug te keren.

Het V.V.V. staat het gehele jaar door tot Uw beschikking voor stadsrondleidingen met gids. Voor nadere inlichtingen gelieve zich in verbinding te stellen met het V.V.V.

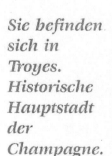

The Town of Troyes

Ah, Troyes! How many times did I hear music in your beautiful churches! You are the town where I was born, the town of my youth, the town which was destined to become an important place. Troyes, the former capital of Champagne, is situated on the River Seine, southeast of Paris. It has a cathedral and churches dating from the thirteenth century. It was in Troyes, in 1420, that the treaty was signed that made Henry V of England the new regent of the kingdom. He was to marry Catherine of France.

a) Find Troyes on a map of France. The town is situated between Paris and Dijon, in the region of Champagne. (They tell me that the word *champagne* is well known in your century.) With a friend, find out some information about the area. Take notes on the relief, climate, vegetation, natural resources and population distribution. Prepare an interesting and well-documented piece of work, with maps, diagrams and drawings. Do not forget you are discovering all about my native land!

b) What a difference between Troyes, the town of my birth, and Ville-Marie, the little town where I was to spend the greater part of my life! Can you try to find out what those differences were, my dear student? Write them down, in two columns, and do not forget to indicate the similarities also (there were more than you think, you know).

c) Imagine the open-air market in the Troyes of the seventeenth century. Can you hear the shouts of the stallholders and the noises of the animals? Can you see all the different produce, and all the multi-coloured fabrics? Can you smell the pungent odours in the air? Form a group with several friends, and, together, recreate a market scene on a lovely spring day. Stage it (remember to rehearse it well!), and present it to the class. Remember that you are in *my* century.

Marguerite Bourgeoys, Canada's first school mistress teaching sewing at the Industrial School which she organized at Montreal in 1665.

The Seventeenth Century

Let's go from the market in Troyes to an overall view of France in the seventeenth century. There were of course many other interesting countries in the world; I knew only France and New France. There were many countries where the white man and woman had never set foot, and where fine and rich civilizations flourished.

In France, the century started with Louis XIII's accession to the throne in 1610. Cardinal Richelieu, an intelligent, ambitious and powerful man headed the government from 1624-1642. The following year, Louis XIII died. His young son, Louis XIV, was only five years old. As he grew into the role of king, he assumed more and more power, until finally he assumed total power and called himself a ruler by divine right. During his reign France knew glory. However, the country soon fell into an economic decline.

a) In the library you will find details on civilizations — from all over the world — that flourished in the seventeenth century. Choose four of them. Compare them, noting their similarities and differences under the titles: place, type of government, principal cultural aspects, economy. Add other titles if you need to.

b) Prepare a debate with a friend who does not share your opinion on the advantages and disadvantages of seventeenth century life. Each of you will present his or her point of view to the rest of the class. It will decide the winner by vote. Don't forget such aspects as housing, food, education, clothing and entertainment — everything we call the customs or the ways of a people.

c) You are a writer. You are writing a story based on the life of a child of the seventeenth century. Whether he or she be Native American, Chinese, African, or of any other racial group, you will try to imagine his or her particular situation, and write about it.

An Italian seventeenth century lute labelled Jacobus Anellus de Boctis 1674

Paul de Chomedey de Maisonneuve
1612-1676

Sieur de Maisonneuve, who founded the settlement of Ville-Marie in 1642, was a nobleman, soldier and believer. He neither took nor accepted one arpent[*] of land in New France. He was just, sincere and thoughtful. His joy was to serve God and his country, his pleasure to make music. It was the Jesuit superior Charles Lalemant who had introduced Monsieur de Maison-neufve to Monsieur de la Dauversière. (Maison-neufve was the seventeenth century spelling of his name.) Monsieur de la Dauversière had the idea of founding Ville-Marie after a discussion with the abbot Jean-Jacques Olier. He was searching for a young, religious man capable of directing such a project when Paul de Chomedey entered the picture. He was just the man he had been looking for. Paul de Chomedey de Maisonneade arrived in New France in 1641, a few weeks after the arrival of Jeanne Mance. He met with severe opposition in Québec where they thought that founding a settlement like Ville-Marie was a bad idea. But he was not a man to be easily put off: true to his task, he succeeded in persuading Governor de Monmagny to let him colonize the Île de Montréal.

The books written by the Jesuits, the *Jesuit Relations*, are filled with details of daily life in Ville-Marie. They mention the cross Maisonneuve erected on top of Mount Royal. They speak of the lands he granted, and the position of governor of the colony he refused. They refer also to the constant danger the Iroquois presented as the original inhabitants of the land. In 1651, Maisonneuve went back to France to recruit 200 men to form a militia in Ville-Marie. It was in the year 1655 that I set foot on this land that seemed to draw me to it. Twelve years later, our dear governor of Ville-Marie, a victim of intrigue, was recalled to France by an ungrateful administration that did not know how to reward him for his good and loyal services. He finished his days in Paris, a just and humble man, his heart filled with the memories of those 23 years he had spent working tirelessly in Ville-Marie, on the Île de Montréal. He did not play his lute again.

a) You are Sieur de Maisonneuve, my dear student. How lucky you are! What you are trying to accomplish in Ville-Marie is very difficult. Write a simple and precise report to the French government detailing the hardships of each day, the lack of supplies, and the ever-present danger of the Native peoples. Use calligraphy if possible to give your report the style of our time.

b) In a group, discuss what you think was important to Sieur de Maisonneuve, and by the same token, what was unimportant to him. What do you think of his priorities?

---

[*] We are speaking here of about one acre, or roughly 3,400m², as you say in your time. The arpent was the standard measure of land with us, and is still used in Quebec and Louisiana in your day.

The Trades

I mentioned that Paul de Chomedey de Maisonneuve played the lute. In the seventeenth century, as in your century, music was a great source of enjoyment and entertainment. However, the professional musician was very poorly paid. What happens in your time? I have heard that a celebrity can earn huge sums of money. When I was a little girl, people had to work at certain trades or professions to make a reasonable living; many of those occupations would have been different from the ones you know now.

The following is a list of the trades to be found in 1665-1666:

Trade	Count	Trade	Count
Aiguiseur d'épées — sword sharpener	1	Fabricant de chandelles — candle-maker	3
Armurier — armourer	4	Ferblantier — tinsmith	1
Arquebusier — gunsmith	7	Fondeur — founder	1
Bailli — bailiff	4	Gentilhomme — nobleman	16
Bijoutier — jeweller	1	Imprimeur — printer	1
Boucher — butcher	7	Instituteur — teacher	3
Boulanger — baker	11	Jardinier — gardener	3
Brasseur — brewer	1	Maçon — mason	32
Briquetier — brick maker	1	Manchonnier — sleeve maker	1
Capitaine de navire — ship's captain	1	Marchand — shopkeeper	18
Chapelier — hatter	7	Matelot — sailor	32
Charpentier — carpenter	36	Menuisier — joiner	27
Charron — wheelwright	2	Meunier — miller	9
Chaudronnier — brazier	3	Notaire — notary	3
Chirurgien — surgeon	5	Sabotier — clog maker	1
Charbonnier — collier	1	Sellier — saddler	3
Cloutier — nail maker	4	Serrurier — locksmith	3

Confiseur — confectioner	5	Taillandier — edge-tool maker	14
Cordier — rope maker	6	Tailleur de pierre — stonecutter	1
Cordonnier — shoemaker	20	Tailleur — tailor	30
Corroyeur — currier	8	Tisserand — weaver	16
Coutelier — cutler	1	Tisserand de tapis — carpet weaver	3
Couvreur — roofer	1	Tonnelier — cooper	8
Domestique — servant	401	Tourneur — turner	1
Drapier — draper	4		
Fabricant de boutons — button maker	1	Total:	763

a)   Which one of those trades would you have chosen? Why? Reply in writing, all the while considering your talents and tastes, and the pastimes you prefer.

b)   My father was a master candle-maker and coiner at the Mint in Troyes — two demanding trades. Write a letter to the Royal Canadian Mint in Ottawa asking for information about the type of work performed there and the conditions of employment. Remember that the form of the letter is important as it is a business letter. Write neatly, precisely and concisely.

c)   The phrase "master candle-maker" sounds quite grand. My brother and I soon discovered that selling candles did not bring the same glory, but we did it anyway. Think of other trades which would be valued highly in my time. Make a list of them. Have each member of your group choose one, and prepare a lesson that he or she would teach to his or her apprentices.

d)   Do you have an artistic talent, my dear student? Design a series of six postage stamps representing various trades from the seventeenth century. Send a copy to the head office of the Canada Post. (I believe that is what you call the service in your time.)

Coronation of the Virgin. Devotional and philosophical writings, London, c. 1325-1335.

Mysticism

In a way, stamps are symbols representing different aspects of the life of a people, country, nation or state. One aspect of *my* life was what some call mysticism, the philosophical belief that aims at the close union of human being and God. It claims that perfection can be found in the contemplation of a symbol of the divinity. I myself have had experiences of this kind, to the point that I could not doubt the existence of God. The most striking event in my spiritual life took place in 1640, when the power and the love of the Holy Mother were revealed to me in all their splendour and glory.

a) Have you had a similar experience, my dear student? If the reply is yes, describe it in your personal journal; if no, ask some older friends, and you will probably find enough to write a whole story.

b) It is said that the organ is a church instrument. We played it in my time, in France. I would like you to find some organ music, and to pick a piece that would go with my mystic enlightenment in front of the church at Troyes. Play the tape and read the passage from the text with it. Read with precision and feeling. Lower the lights to create the appropriate atmosphere.

c) Do some research on famous mystics of several religions. Make a presentation to the class on the one who interests you the most. As you write, ask yourself the following questions: do you admire him or her? Was his or her life changed by a special event? Could this person convince you to believe or act like him or her? What would have happened to him or her without the intervention of mysticism?

SAINT HUGH OF GRENOBLE VISITING THE REFECTORY. About 1633. Seville, Museum

Our Religious Order — Les congrégantines

Spain and France had a great number of mystics and religious thinkers in the seventeenth century. Our order followed their teaching very closely. However, the external branch of this order, out working in the community, was a movement that supported change. It embraced new and contemporary thought. Mother Louise de Sainte-Marie was at our head. She was the older sister of Paul de Chomedey de Maisonneuve and one of his inheritors in 1676. I myself belonged to this movement and supported it with deep devotion.

a) We were laywomen. Explain in writing what differences existed between us, who were the teachers who worked in the town, and the members of the cloistered religious orders who did not have either the wish or the right to go out into the world.

b) Draw up a list of different Christian orders (nuns and monks). Classify them according to their country of origin, patron saint, doctrine and rules.

c) Prepare a debate on the advantages and disadvantages of a cloistered life in comparison to one that is more open (when speaking of religious orders). Choose a partner who holds your opinion and two others who do not. Go to it resolutely! I shall listen to you with great interest, because I hold a strong opinion on this subject.

A Dutch sailing vessel of the mid-seventeenth century

Jacob A. Bellevois (1621 - 1676) Gomshall Gallery, Gomshall-Surrey
Schepen voor de haven van Vlissingen (detail) / Shipping outside Flushing harbour (detail) /
Schiffe vor dem Hafen von Vlissingen (Ausschnitt) / Des bateaux devant le port de Flessengue
(détail) / Barcos fuera del puerto de Flesinga (detalle)

Sailing Ships

Well, my dear student, I certainly had plenty of contact with the real world. At the age of 33, I found myself in mid-ocean aboard a ship bound for New France. What a journey! What an adventure! Unfortunately, I did not have good sea legs. The ship took eight weeks to reach land, and each day of each week passed in an unending succession of trials and tribulations.

a) You are the French captain of my sailing vessel. Imagine that at the outset of the crossing, you and your crew give your passengers a tour of the ship. To prepare yourself for this, look for some information (with illustrations) on the ships of my time. Create a skit which you will present to the whole class. Choose a corner of the classroom where you and your crew will have the space to make your imaginary vessel.

b) And now, you are my shipboard companion. Each day you write in your diary, telling about the fortunate and unfortunate happenings that take place during the crossing. Write two passages, one on a calm sunny day, and the other during a frightening storm. If you use light brown paper and try to write in the script of my time, you will have a diary which is both readable and true to the period.

c) Draw a sailing ship of my era. Pay attention to the dimensions! Under your drawing, make a cross-section of the vessel. Indicate all the necessary details on both drawings.

The home of Jeanne Mance – the first Hôtel-Dieu, Ville-Marie, 1645

Ville-Marie

We disembarked at Québec. The sailing ship, our refuge for eight long weeks, stayed there in the port. The remainder of the journey was done by canoe. At this time, Ville-Marie was a little fortified village built for the missionaries. It had a solid palisade, which is a row of strong, pointed, wooden stakes placed closely together. I heard that later on, Ville-Marie was going to become a large fur-trading centre. On fair days, the Native people and the merchants would meet at Ville-Marie to exchange their goods — the merchants bringing guns, tools and brandy, and the Native people their furs. These fairs would begin with the smoking of the peace pipe, but trickery, profit and loss were common currency all the same at the heart of this little world.

a)   I have heard it said that a large city is to be found today on the site of Ville-Marie. Do you know this city? Find it on a map. Describe the advantages and disadvantages of living in this city in your time rather than in the little village of the seventeenth century.

b)   Ville-Marie: there's a different sort of name! Why was this parcel of land given this name? What do you think? With your friends, discuss the significance of this name, then invent your own name for this village. Do the same for New France. Draw up a list of all the names which were suggested by the groups.

c)   "The situation of Ville-Marie, on an island in a river, had a decisive influence on its growth." What do you think about that? Imagine that you are a history teacher. With the help of maps and precise diagrams, give a strong and relevant presentation that will try to prove the truth of this statement, or prove otherwise, depending on your opinion.

Jeanne Mance

Jeanne Mance
1606-1673

Ville-Marie was where my new acquaintance lived. She was Jeanne Mance. The hospital she ran with her nurses was one of the rare stone buildings in the village. She had given herself the sole task of curing the sick. She had been practising this profession, or rather the art of nursing, since her youth in Langres, in the Champagne region. In her youth, too, she had been an avid listener to the stories being told about New France. She decided to go to this land which she had imagined as quite wonderful. First she had to ask permission from her priest; that was granted. While in Paris, waiting to have her affairs put in order, she became acquainted with people of the nobility — *personnes de qualité* — who suggested that she should build a hospital, the Hôtel-Dieu, in Ville-Marie. The necessary funds for this project would be supplied by Madame de Bullion and Madame la Duchesse d'Aiguillon.

In her position as member of the society of *Notre-Dame de Montréal*, Jeanne had certain powers when she disembarked at Québec on August 8, 1641. The hospital, the Hôtel-Dieu, was founded the next year. However, things did not go as well as expected. In 1651, the Iroquois concentrated their efforts on Ville-Marie — the Huron people having been almost annihilated — and it was Jeanne Mance who saved the situation by giving 22,000 pounds to M. de Maisonneuve so that he could return to France to recruit 200 men. (She had received the money from her benefactors.) In my opinion, this gesture saved Ville-Marie.

In 1658, I accompanied my friend to France, where she had to go for a cure. (The journey had the further aim of giving back the Île de Montréal to the Sulpicians, the order founded in 1644 by Father Olier.) From 1663 on, Louis XIV brought about great changes in New France, but both Jeanne Mance and M. de Maisonneuve had great difficulty trying to enlighten him on the difficult situation that existed there.

a) Compare the conditions you find in a modern hospital to those which the Hôtel-Dieu hospital in Ville-Marie would have had to offer. Think of all the aspects involved, and express yourself clearly and precisely in writing, because what you have to say will greatly interest my companion, Jeanne.

b) Jeanne Mance was an excellent role model for the people in her community. Can you think of three people of your time of whom you could say the same? In a group, discuss their contributions on a local, national or international scale, and state why their influence is a good one.

Étable-école de Marguerite Bourgeoys   1658   Marguerite Bourgeoys's Stable-School

A Stable — A School

Very near the hospital there was a stable made of stone. My friend, Sieur de Maisonneuve, knew well that my greatest desire at that time was to have my own little school, where I could teach on a regular basis. So, he made me a present of this stable, and it turned out that what had been intended as a shelter for animals became a centre of learning for human beings. This school did not resemble yours, my dear student. It comprised one room on the bottom and an attic up above, which you had to reach by an outside stair. My teaching assistants and myself, along with the little girl I had adopted, lived in the attic, its hard floor notwithstanding. Underneath was my classroom.

a)   Imagine yourself a pupil in my school (a girl, as it is girls I teach). You learn fast, and one day you write a poem dedicated to this stable-school. Write a few verses, dreaming from time to time of those marvellous moments when you would run barefoot in the grass on a beautiful July day.

b)   Now my dear student, you have the opportunity to be able to examine the differences and the similarities between your school and mine. Make a written comparison for me, as the profession of teaching has always been dear to my heart.

c)   Imagine something exciting or frightening that could have happened in my school — and we all know it happened often! It could have been a fire, for example, or an attack by the Iroquois, or even (less serious, but leaving a lasting impression all the same) the unexpected visit of a high-ranking administrator. Distribute the roles among your friends and do a little play-acting.

Christ in Glory. Psalter, England, c. 1170.

The Journey to France

No dramatic event could equal the wondrous miracle that took place in France on my visit there. As you know, I had accompanied Jeanne Mance, who had gone to France in search of a cure, as she was very ill. The fact is that something extraordinary happened, a supernatural event occurred quite simply and without ceremony, when she touched the reliquary of Jean-Jacques Olier. Her profound faith and her strong focus had brought about one of the greatest miracles I had ever seen.

a) Do you believe in miracles? Are there events that take place in this world which cannot be explained? You have to prepare a program for television news, an interesting and well-documented program on something mysterious that has happened somewhere in the world of your century. Do your research well, because thousands of viewers will be watching!

b) On our return journey, we were accompanied by the confessor to the nurses of the Hôtel-Dieu Hospital, and three French women who were going to assist me in my duties. Assume the role of one of these four people and write a letter of farewell to a relative or friend in France explaining the reasons for your departure for New France.

*Marguerite Bourgeoys — from the Marguerite Bourgeoys Cultural Centre,
38, rue Georges Clemenceau, 10000 Troyes, France*

1670 — In France Once Again

You have just written a letter to your parents or best friend. For my part, I was going to France once again to receive very special letters, letters issued by royal decree, publicly according me a favour — *lettres patentes*. Monseigneur François de Laval, Bishop of New France, had liked the system of education that I had put into place in Ville-Marie. So, I had decided to take the risk of going to see King Louis XIV himself. It was an experience I shall not forget.

Up until February 24, 1663, New France had been run by a company —the *Compagnie des Cent Associés*. Now, it was the Crown that ruled over New France. It was Louis XIV, who had decreed himself ruler by divine right, who was henceforth going to manage our colony. The worshipping of His Majesty, the passive obedience surrounding him, and the centralization of power had weakened the French nobility however. "The reign of Louis XIV has been very long — 1643-1715 — and although it has been magnificent, it has brought ruin to the country." I had heard these words from many sources.

a) Read the parts from my first story that tell about my voyages. As you can guess, everything that happened to me had a great effect on me. Try now to recreate these scenes, feeling my enthusiasm, determination and joy. Write a passage about this, as if I were writing it. I shall be very curious to see the results of your work.

b) Find some information on the following historical persons: Jeanne Mance, Monseigneur François de Montmorency-Laval, Jean Talon, Jean-Baptiste Colbert and Louis XIV. Have each member of your group who did some research choose his or her favourite person and then try to take on his or her personality, responsibilities and way of life. You must then present these characters to the class without forgetting, of course, that they are people of the seventeenth century.

c) I used the term *lettres patentes*. Think of a patent that has been granted to an inventor, like the one granted to me for my educational system. Now, *you* invent something: a machine, a game, a technique... Make a model or draw a design of your invention. Write to the patent or copyright office describing it in detail. This is a business letter, so use the correct form.

English words by Alan Mills

Gently

Ho,   Ho,   Wa - ta - nay,   Ho,   Ho,   Wa - ta - nay,
Sleep, sleep, lit - tle one, Sleep, sleep, lit - tle one,

Ho,   Ho,   Wa - ta - nay, Ki - yo - ke - na, Ki - yo - ke - na.
Sleep, sleep, lit - tle one, Now go to sleep, now go to sleep.

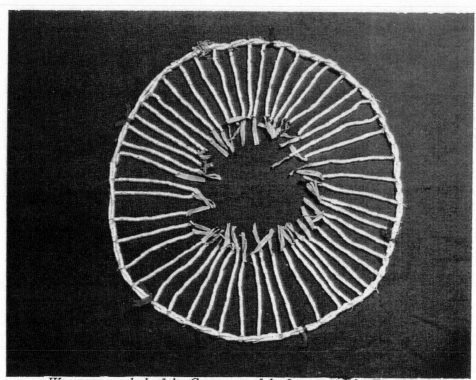

Wampum symbol of the Covenant of the League of the Five Nations

The Native Peoples

The Native peoples had lived on this land we called New France for many hundreds of years. They were at one with their environment, if not with each other. Our presence, becoming ever more powerful, was a threat to many of them. They in turn proved a threat to us. The danger brought on by the Iroquois attacks forced us to find a means of survival. The Hurons, our allies, had fought the Iroquois continuously, but the latter almost annihilated them in 1650. Both the dislike that existed between these two peoples and the rivalry between the French and the English had taken some very violent turns. After defeating the Hurons, the Iroquois threw the responsibility onto the French, who had kept them back from the important business of trafficking in furs.

a)   The Hurons and the *Français* were allied for business reasons and for war: in fact, they had been friends since the arrival of Samuel de Champlain. Try to state the reasons for such a friendship and mutual respect in one paragraph. Don't forget to mention the work of the coureurs de bois and the missionaries; without them, New France would have been very different.

b)   At your public library you might find a map showing the territories of the Native peoples in my time. Try to draw one, clearly indicating the name of the inhabitants with their principal customs and ways of life.

c)   Have a debate (after some good preparation) about the situation of the Native peoples in *your* century. Choose someone who is of your opinion for your debating team, and two friends of a different opinion to oppose you. Speak with knowledge and passion.

The arrival of filles du Roi in the colony

Les filles du Roi — Daughters of the King

One of the French political decisions that benefitted the whole colony was that of sending to New France young women of marrying age, orphans, raised at the expense of the State by religious women's orders. The King acted for them as fathers did for their daughters in my time. It was the project of Louis XIV, Jean-Baptiste Colbert and Jean Talon, the famous intendant. After a few preliminary difficulties, things seemed to go along well. Almost 1,000 filles du Roi arrived in New France between 1665 and 1673. The colonists were encouraged to come and choose a wife from among them. As every man who was not married had to pay a tax, and moreover, as married couples with several children received subsidies, bachelors became quite rare in the colony. Indeed, the filles du Roi found husbands very quickly, even if the reality did not always conform to the dream they had had of married life.

a) The expansion of the colony was almost guaranteed by this idea of sending women across the ocean to settle in New France. The women were between the ages of 16 and 40. I was the one who questioned each man who wished to choose a companion. Write a dialogue between a young soldier who has come in search of a wife, and me, who questions him carefully: on his health, wealth, ambitions and desires. After writing the dialogue, stage it with the help of a friend.

b) You are a fille du Roi. Your journey has been entirely paid for by the State. You have spent two months aboard a little sailing ship. You have disembarked. One week has passed and you are writing the first page of your diary. I hope you will like your new country as much as I do.

c) Make a list of the qualities — moral and physical — that were necessary in a fille du Roi for her to have a fair chance of success and happiness in this new land. You can also say what you think about the categories already proposed: *Petiz et grans et beaulx et laidz.*

Première chapelle   Notre-Dame-de-Bon-Secours, 1678 First Chapel

Notre-Dame-de-Bonsecours, the 'sailors' chapel'

The Chapel of Bonsecours

Success, that is what I finally had with the building of my dear chapel of Notre-Dame-de-Bon-Secours — the first stone church erected on the Île de Montréal! After all the delays, the unforeseen events, the false starts, I could see this building take shape and give itself over to the service of God. I had desired this for so long.

a)   I heard that a building of the same name exists in your century on the site of the first chapel or very near to it. Can you find it on a map? Learn about its history through the centuries and the uses it has been put to. Give a presentation to the class on this subject, illustrating it with pictures (photographs, postcards or slides).

b)   Since ancient times, human beings have built structures to the glory of the gods and spirits they honoured: perhaps they placed stones one atop the other (like the dolmens, the menhirs or Stonehenge), or perhaps they erected magnificent temples and cathedrals. Find 10 of such structures from around the world, and classify them under the headings: religion, country, date, reason for construction.

c)   Write two paragraphs on the importance of places of worship (church, temple, mosque, synagogue, for example). Compare their importance in your century to that of the seventeenth century. Has the situation changed greatly, from your point of view? Think long and hard about that question, because there could be many reasons for such a change. Become both a historian and a philosopher!

The sisters of the order of the Congregation of Notre-Dame

Religion and Education

According to me, religion and education are almost inseparable. The order of the Congregation of Notre-Dame, founded in 1598 in France, still retains this close bond in your century. This order, which we introduced to Ville-Marie in the seventeenth century, was going to spread throughout the entire world: in your day it is well-known and well respected. Another order, the Ursuline, directed in Québec by Sister Marie de l'Incarnation (Marie Guyart), founded a nunnery and a boarding school for girls in that town. In the many letters she wrote to her family and religious friends in France, Sister Marie describes how, in her opinion, religion was closely bound to education. It must be noted however that the Ursulines were cloistered, and as such could not go out into the world to practise their doctrine, while *our* order remained open to all the events of the century.

a) Do some research on the order to which I belonged, the order of Notre-Dame. It exists in your century in many French-speaking countries. Can you name some? Write a paragraph on the reasons why it has survived for 400 years, according to you.

b) The name of this order was chosen with care — Notre-Dame. Discuss this choice with your group, and suggest other names that would have been both logical and meaningful. I hope the names are such that I won't blush over your judgment!

c) I was beatified then canonized in the twentieth century. What an honour! Look up the meaning of these two words (beatify and canonize), and as editor-in-chief of the official Vatican newspaper, write an account of these decisions taken by the Pope and his counsellors. I hope you think that I have deserved this double honour. *Au revoir*, my dear student.

Marguerite Bourgeoys

Jean Talon

Québec,
le 16 juillet 1671

Dear Reader,

My name is Jean Talon. I am sure that my story is going to captivate you and help you live the dream of your life in the colony of New France, this colony which is so dear to all of us. Your energy and passion will remain with you as you discover and help build this new land. Our faithful companions en route will be initiative, vitality and tenacity, all at their peak. Come and see the wharf crowded with people and laden with provisions; come and feel the hustle and bustle; come and listen to the workmen's hammers as they build this land. Everything is going beautifully in our colony, and it's up to us to be a support for its growth and its flourishing!

Your most devoted intendant,

Jean Talon

Jean Talon
1625 -1694

Would that be New France that is calling out for me so urgently? Well, if that is the case, I reply with all my heart: *"Présent!"*

My dear readers, *bonjour*! Allow me to introduce myself: my name is Jean Talon du Quesnoy, Comte d'Orsainville. I am going to paint you a colourful picture of the New France I knew during my stay there, from 1665-1672.

Like Monsieur de Maisonneuve, Mesdemoiselles Jeanne Mance and Marguerite Bourgeoys, I come from the province of Champagne, in France, a prodigious province I am sure you will agree! I received my education in Paris at the Jesuit College of Clermont. I was a good student, ambitious and creative; my teachers said that one of my talents was the ability to form very clear ideas. I could "conceptualize" from my experiences, they said. In truth, when I think back on the tasks I had to accomplish in New France, I can see that this particular talent served me well. I was young when I entered the world of the French administration. Thanks to my abundant energy and my practicality, I was given the position of war commissioner in Flanders. Then, I became the intendant of the province of Hainaut in northeastern France. My life as a high-ranking bureaucrat had begun.

Here I was at 40 years of age, wondering where my profession would lead me, when lo and behold! I was appointed to the post of intendant of our colony across the sea, New France. They chose *me*! And who chose me? It was the Sun King himself — the *Roi-Soleil* — the great Louis XIV, on the advice of his finance minister Jean-Baptiste Colbert. Jean-Baptiste Colbert was the most intelligent, demanding and clear-sighted individual in the royal government; he was soon to become secretary of state. And he had chosen me!

On the 24ᵗʰ of May, I found myself on board the good ship *Saint-Sébastien* accompanied by the new governor of the colony Monsieur Rémy de Courcelles. The voyage was long enough, as you can imagine — even for a patient man like myself. Québec* welcomed us on the 12ᵗʰ of September in the year of grace 1665.

"Ah, there he is at last, he's disembarking. They call him Intendant Talon. He's the first intendant to set foot on our soil here in New France. I wonder what *he* thinks he can do for this colony which just survives from day to day."

"What a handsome gentleman! The gods smiled on him when he was born! If he is Talon, I would like to be the *semelle*!"

"Be quiet, Ginette, he's coming this way."

I looked straight into the eyes of this young artisan and the pretty dark-haired girl by his

---

* The word *Québec* comes from the *kebec*, the name the Native peoples had given to the place where the river narrowed. Sieur de Champlain liked the name. To Jacques Cartier it had been the Iroquoian village of Stadacona, 70 years earlier.

side, and there I could see anxiety, not confidence: their worried expressions told me that everything was not right in this "best of new worlds." Very well then, there was work to do! Perhaps I was the right man for the job.

During the autumn I carefully examined the finances of New France. They were in a poor state; its fur trade was suffering at the hands of the Iroquois, and the colonists' enthusiasm was visibly waning. The company that had been running the colony — the *Compagnie des Cent Associés* — was now ruined: the colony had become a royal possession. The grand plans of King Louis XIV and M. Colbert to reorganize New France had to be carried out, and carried out well. I know I am a man of imagination, and resourcefulness; I am open-minded and quick-witted, so I believe I am up to the task. If I do pay great attention to details, I am also capable of seeing the whole picture: as you know, the whole is usually more than the sum of its parts.

To work! Where did I put M. Colbert's notes, with their rules and regulations and so on? Ah, here they are.

Point number 1: "The Governor's powers will be reduced." Oh dear! That will not make me very popular with His Excellency. He will take care of "military affairs, Native affairs, the English colonies, the religious orders and education" (all told that is not so bad). As for me, the Intendant, I have to oversee "the civil administration, the maintenance of law and order, the nomination of judges, the control of finances, the upkeep of fortifications, the taxes, the royal business ventures" — and I have to make sure the Governor assumes *his* responsibilities. That should keep me busy, what do you say?

Point number 2: "The Sovereign Council, the highest court in the land, will help mete out justice and put in place an administrative body." Hold on a moment, here is a clever move by Monsieur Colbert: he wants "five councillors from among the most influential colonists in the country to be nominated by the Governor, the Bishop and the Intendant." I know the civil powers are losing their authority over the ordinary people, and even the Church has difficulty in this regard — that is worrying.

Point number 3: "The West India* Company will keep its seigneurial, property, and judiciary rights," but it is the King who will hold the reins and control it — I had guessed as much!

Good, now I understand the details of his program. It is up to me to adapt it to the needs of the colony, so wish me luck in this enormous venture! Let's go down to the wharf and hear what the ordinary people are saying.

"My goodness me! The wharf is packed with people! What's going on, Pierre my friend?"

"Look at that! It's the beauties arriving from France, another boatload of filles du Roi. They say there will be more than 1,000 of these young women here in two or three years to help increase the population. And you, Ti-Jean, if you don't marry one of them you'll have to pay a tax to the Intendant, and what's more, he'll take away your rights to hunt and fish. Do you realize that? As for me, my family never stops growing, and when Marie has had her tenth one, I'll get some money from the authorities and maybe an important job as well."

---

* You refer to West India as the Greater and Lesser Antilles, a group of islands forming the greater part of the West Indies.

"I'm just an ordinary farmhand, as you know, Pierre, but I have just one more year to work on this farm, and then I'll have my land, tools and provisions just like you. Maybe then I'll marry one of these *petites blondes*."

"Look, Ti-Jean, here come the recruits from the Carignan-Salières Regiment. Surely they're going to stay in the colony; they've been offered parcels of land. This Intendant Talon is certainly encouraging immigration! They say there'll be more than 7,000 people here in New France by 1672!"

Let us leave these two habitants to their heated discussion. I am going down to the docks now, to the new dry dock built on the St. Charles River. Ah, can you see what I see down there in the graving dock? A fine ship indeed, 500 tonnes* they tell me, built by our carpenters from France. Well, we have the wood here, the hemp for the rigging, and the tar for the ship's protection, so why not have a shipbuilding industry? Down there is the first real dockyard in the colony. I know it is a costly industry, but what must be done must be done, and we just have to be patient and determined. We have already exported ships' masts to France, and barrel staves to West India (where the sugar cane and rum industries need barrels). I am pleased with it all. Now, let us go and see what is happening on the farms.

"Oh, Colette, there is Monsieur l'Intendant and I look a mess!"

"Mesdemoiselles, I wish you a good morning! Is your father out in the fields? I am doing my round of the farms this morning, and the Seigneury of Notre-Dame-des-Anges is one of my favourite projects. I had the idea of putting three villages together, the houses almost touching one another. The land has been well cleared, the farming is good, and you can always count on the services of a priest, a surgeon or a lawyer. It is a parcel of land in the shape of a triangle. But, I am rambling on here. Tell me, Mesdemoiselles, do you grow wheat here?"

"Yes, Monsieur l'Intendant, lots of it; there's even too much for us. The same goes for the peas and beans. Father says we should sell the surplus from our harvest."

"Hold your tongue, Colette! Don't forget you're speaking to Monsieur l'Intendant. Monsieur, it's true that we've had some success here. So have our neighbours the Lemyre, who raise cattle. They have horses and sheep now to add to the cows and pigs."

"And Father has planted flax and hemp too, and even some hops, hops to make beer."

"Ah, yes, hops for the brewery: there is another industry that is going well, since the Sovereign Council limited the imports on alcohol. In the past, we spent more than 100,000 livres on strong liquor, and now here we are making our very own beer, enough for it to be a commercial venture. But I am thinking aloud, my dear young ladies, and boring you with such serious matters. Please tell your father that I am very pleased with the variety of his produce, and that I shall buy his hemp myself as proof of my confidence in him. The rope making industry needs all it can get. But I must get back to town now. Mesdemoiselles, I thank you for your patience and take my humble leave."

"Adieu, Monsieur l'Intendant. Good health!"

---

* We measure a ship's weight or volume in tonnes, according to how much water the ship displaces. In your day you might say "metric tons." Any one unit of them equals 1,000 kg, as you put it.
* A livre was worth a pound of silver to us.

I noticed that those charming young girls were dressed in clothes woven here in Québec. Excellent! There is the beginning of yet another industry — weaving. Even their shoes had been made in the factory in the Lower Town; the tannery at Pointe Lévis provided the leather.

Everything is going well; the economy of the colony is really picking up.

Look over there to the left. It is a little hat factory. I am wearing one of its products, a fine hat of beaver felt. It is well made, too! And look down there — the St. Lawrence River, majestic and tireless in its flow. It is the lifeblood of the colony, you know, the main artery of commerce for New France, France and West India. And let us not forget fishing! I can just see an immense fishing industry develop. In France it is dried cod they eat. Why not sell them fish from Acadie, Gaspésie, and places all down the shore? We can have warehouses in Acadie where we can store our fish for winter, when the river is frozen. There's an idea!

"Ah, come in, Monsieur Godot, I was waiting for you. And as I waited, Godot, I was thinking about the future of our colony. I would like to consult you about this, my surveyor."

"Monsieur l'Intendant, my humble self will try to be worthy of your confidence."

"I see the St. Lawrence River as the real heart of our colony. I am exploring the land to the north, right up to the bay, and to the west to find the passage to China, and to the south as well, as far as we can go. There lies three-quarters of a continent that can become our vast kingdom in this year of grace 1672. What do you think about that?"

"It's a brilliant idea and a practical one, as your ideas always are, if you will permit me to say so, Monsieur l'Intendant. You are no doubt thinking about the mineral resources also, the copper, lead, iron and coal found in abundance. However, we must not forget the Iroquois and the English."

"I know, I know.... But this New France is going to extend itself in all directions, in spite of my shaky relationship with the Governor and the business people of Québec. One is jealous, the others are greedy and incapable, and the Jesuits continue to distrust me and my ideas. Too bad, I say, Rome was not built in a day!"

"Monsieur l'Intendant, what you have done for this colony goes far beyond what was thought possible. I quote Monsieur Colbert in this regard. 'Monsieur Talon is both the architect and the builder of New France, both the theoretician and the pragmatist behind its programs. He is capable of seeing the whole picture; he is a realist even while holding on to his dreams. Powerful in conception, resolute in decision and rapid in execution, he is an intendant without equal.' Such is the high opinion the government of the kingdom holds of you."

"Yes, Monsieur Godot, the King himself was kind enough to express his appreciation of my work. My dream is to see what began as a humble village become a vast empire."

"That will come, Monsieur l'Intendant, that will come."

"Yes, my dear Godot, that will come. We shall speak about this again."

I went back to France in the November of 1672. Louis XIV offered me the posts of secretary of the cabinet and gentleman-in-waiting to His Majesty. I accepted. My years of being New France's intendant, from 1665-1668 and from 1670-1672, had been well appreciated by my native land. I was consultant to Monsieur Colbert and I had the King's ear. Unmarried, rich and respected, I lived on the Rue du Bac in Paris, near the Seine, till my death in November, 1694. My burial took place in Champagne where everything had started. The dream I had had for New France followed me to my grave.

Below: French citizens queue to pay their taxes. Louis' grandiose schemes, and his costly wars in particular, forced him to impose heavy direct taxes on all classes.

The Administration of a Country

I have spent my life in French administrations, first in Flanders and in the province of Hainaut, then in New France, and once more in France with Monsieur Colbert and King Louis XIV at the Palace of Versailles. Do not think, my young friend, that such a career ever lacked interest or vitality. On the contrary! It allowed me to use my imagination to the full. It was Cardinal Richelieu who had had the idea for this new type of administrator called "intendant." At first the idea was badly received because the intendant was going to be too near the seat of royal power. However, this position of intendant ended up as a very important one in the country's administration. Among his duties were the inspection of prisons, the review of soldiers, the maintenance of law and order, the care of roads, canals and mines, the collection of taxes and the protection of the underprivileged in the society. That was a lot of work!

a) Imagine that at the tender age of 30 you become, as I did, an intendant of a province in France. What qualities would you have to have to succeed in your undertaking? Give an example of a situation where one or another of those qualities would be put to the test.

b) You are an intendant in New France. Each month you have to write a report to the secretary of state. This report must be written precisely and concisely, and must present the results of all activities undertaken during the past month.

c) In a group, write and present a skit depicting a situation where there has been an abuse of power by a low-ranking official; the victim has submitted a complaint to the intendant of the colony. Think about all the aspects of the case because *you* are going to have to make the judgment as the intendant.

And now let us go to New France together! Keep an open mind and a probing one, and always remember that the whole is more than the sum of its parts.

133

Superius

Bel le qui tiens ma vi e Cap ti ve dans tes

yeulx   Qui m'as l'a me ra ui e D'un soubz riz

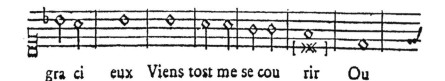

gra ci eux   Viens tost me se cou rir   Ou

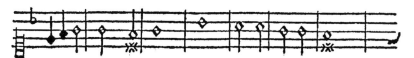

me faul dra mou rir   Viens toft me fecou rir

Ou me faul dra mou rir

CHANSON [a]

Belle qui tiens ma vie
Captive dans tes yeux,
Qui m'as l'âme ravie
D'un souris gracieux,
Viens tôt me secourir
Ou me faudra mourir.

Pourquoi fuis tu, mignarde,
Si je suis près de toi
Quand tes yeux je regarde
Je me perds dedans moi,
Car tes perfections
Changent mes actions.

Mon âme voulait être
Libre de passion,
Mais l'amour s'est fait maître
De mes affections
Et a mis sous sa loi
Et mon coeur et ma foi.

This pavane can be found in the Orchésographie *of Thoinot Arbeau, a canon of Langres in eastern France. (His name on the title page is an anagram of his true name — Jehan Tabourot.) The* Orchésographie *was published in 1589.*

The Music of the Seventeenth Century

Folk music can entertain us, accompany our manual tasks, and evoke memories of our family and native land. We can imagine we hear the sounds of the fiddler playing his dance tunes. His jigs are so enticing that the dancers just leap to their feet.

There are many other types of music I like, the dances at the Palace of Versailles for example, the pavanes, galliards, minuets and sarabands. I like beautiful church music also, and I admire the works of Monsieur Lully, composer, violinist, dancing master to the King, and Director of the Royal Academy of Music in Paris. I must not forget the lovely songs of Janequin — his "Cris de Paris," and his "Chants des Oiseaux" — which charmed Paris in the sixteenth century. You can see that I enjoy the music of my time.

a)   What kind of music do you like? I am sure your tastes will differ greatly from mine. Have your group listen to your favourite piece. Prepare a small presentation on its content and musical form. I too shall listen to it with great interest!

b)   Write a simple, tuneful melody. Tape it and give it as a present to a friend.

c)   Do some research on a composer of the fifteenth, sixteenth, or seventeenth century. That is the era called the Renaissance; it is also the beginning of the Baroque period. Find out about his or her life, his or her native land, the kind of music he or she wrote, and the instruments used at that time. Ask yourself if this composer knew success during his or her lifetime. If the answer is yes, has this fame continued till the twenty-first century? If the answer is no, is your present-day audience now appreciating his or her music and helping to make up for the past?

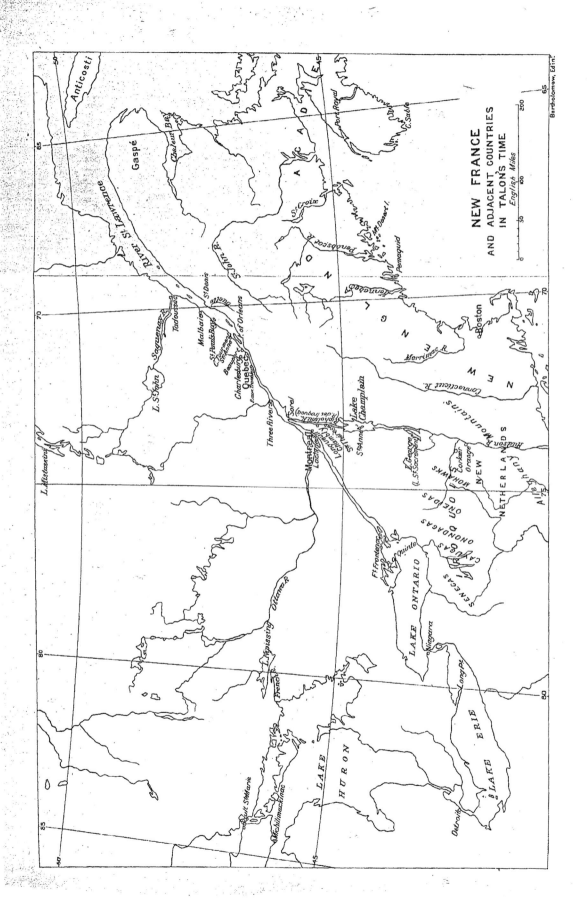

NEW FRANCE
AND ADJACENT COUNTRIES
IN TALON'S TIME

English Miles

Bartholomew, Edin.

The Expansion of the Colony

I would like history to see me as the main instrument in the expansion of New France in the third quarter of the seventeenth century. I am not being arrogant here; I am just looking at things as they were. Our dear colony, which represented the French possessions in North America, had already undergone many painful trials during its short existence. The ever-threatening presence of the English and the Dutch to the south, not to mention that of the Iroquois nearby, made our very existence problematic. To help us through these difficulties we worked hard at building the economy of the colony. We tried to build a solid base for our budding commerce and industry. New France would no longer be a country surviving from day to day; I had made up my mind about that. With my practical ideas, my boundless energy and my wide imagination, I knew I was capable of carrying out the orders of Louis XIV and Jean-Baptiste Colbert.

a) You are the founder and president of a weekly newspaper published in Québec in 1671. In a group, choose a head of production, an editor-in-chief, two journalists and two graphic artists. Your team is going to produce a paper which is both informative and attractive. Don't forget interesting headlines, newsworthy titles and striking illustrations.

b) You have just arrived in New France as a fille du Roi or as an officer in the Carignan-Salières Regiment. Write a letter to your family in France describing the crossing, your first impressions of life in the colony, and your new acquaintances.

c) Find a map of New France. Study it carefully, and draw one similar to it with the compass points, scale and legend. Pay attention to the accuracy of the outline.

LVDOVICVS XIV D. G.
FRANCIÆ ET NAVARRÆ
REX CHRISTIANISSIMVS

LOUIS XIV • *King of France* • *Sept. 5, 1638 – Sept. 1, 1715*

Louis XIV, King of France
1638-1715

I knew King Louis XIV well! Ah, how he could dance — and make his court dance also! I tried to please him in everything I did for New France, and I know he always appreciated my efforts. At the death of his father, Louis XIII, in 1643, the little king was only five years old: at that time I was an 18-year-old student. It was his mother who assumed the regency of course, and M. Mazarin who ran the affairs of state. When M. Mazarin died in 1661, Louis XIV began to put his own mark on the throne: he was an absolute monarch, soon to assume the title of ruler by divine right.

Thanks to the intelligence and clear-sightedness of his new minister of finance, M. Jean-Baptiste Colbert, the economic situation in France, disastrous before, was turned around. The King installed himself in the Palace of Versailles in 1682, 10 years after my return to France. He would have liked to have ruled over the whole of Europe; he engaged in several wars to try to accomplish this. These wars gave him glory, but hurt the country badly in the long-term. Also, the worshipping of the King and the passive obedience of the nobles both helped weaken France.

Louis XIV's reign was long and glorious — from 1643-1715 — and I myself, Intendant Talon, played a certain part in the making of it. But alas, all this grandeur and magnificence was costly for the kingdom.

a) Put together some interesting and accurate information on the reign of Louis XIV (*le Grand*) — the *Roi-Soleil*. Prepare a presentation on both the positive and negative aspects of his reign. As you have a good vantage point from your twenty-first century position, you should be able to give a balanced point of view. Rehearse your presentation and deliver it to the class.

b) You are a critic of French politics between the years 1661 and 1715. Your views are published in a Parisian magazine read by the intellectuals of the time. Write one of your weekly articles suggesting projects, enterprises and goals more suitable to the France of that period.

c) The Palace of Versailles, hallmark of French talent and artistry in the seventeenth century, is the magnificent residence of the King and his court. Its halls and gardens resound with music and laughter. Find out about Versailles and write a poem dedicated to this life of luxury. Record your work against a background of music of the period. (Look in your library for cassettes.)

d) I hear that in your time there are many different types of government. With the help of a friend, choose six countries that you will classify according to the following categories: name of country, standard of living, type of government.

Jean-Baptiste Colbert, 1619-1683

Jean-Baptiste Colbert
1619-1683

Jean-Baptiste Colbert was born in Reims, in the province of Champagne, six years before my own birth in Châlons-sur-Marne in the same province. (Champagne produced several important people for France and New France.) Monsieur Colbert was undoubtedly one of the best ministers France ever had. He contributed to the disgrace and fall of Nicolas Fouquet who was condemned for having squandered the riches of the state, and who was imprisoned for life. M. Colbert became the minister responsible for building, then, a watchful comptroller of finance, and lastly, an excellent secretary of state. There is not an area in public administration where he did not have a great influence. He was in favour of industry and commerce; he reorganized finances, the judicial system and the navy. Moreover, there is a great resemblance between his projects for France and those created for New France. M. Colbert also encouraged the development of arts and letters. He tried to limit the excessive spending of Louis XIV who was too concerned with his own glory and the splendour of Versailles.

a) In a group, create an interesting and well-documented skit about a meeting of the King, M. Colbert and me. We are discussing the future of New France.

b) You are the private secretary of Jean-Baptiste Colbert. Write a pen portrait of this influential minister, and show it to me. I want to compare it to the one I made of him.

c) Name three people from your time who play a significant role in the government or administration of their respective countries. Describe one of the most important aspects of their policies.

Sailing Ships

Transportation played a fundamental role in the economic and political surge of our colony. I found myself aboard the *Saint-Sébastien* on May 24, 1665, bound for New France. The crossing turned out to be longer than usual because we made a stop in Gaspésie to pick up some lead samples. Our little ship reached the port of Québec on the 12th of September.

a) Draw a sailing ship from my era. Under your drawing, make a cross-section of this fine vessel, being careful of the dimensions. Mark all the important details in the two drawings, naming them accurately (Consult a good illustrated dictionary for this; you will probably find one in the library.) I hope you have found your sea legs.

b) Without such means of transportation — the sailing ships — the fascinating explorations of my time would never have taken place. Make a list of famous explorers of the fifteenth, sixteenth, and seventeenth centuries using the following categories: name, nationality, dates of the voyages, departure point, areas discovered or explored.

c) Imagine yourself captain of a three-masted sailing ship of the seventeenth century. You keep a log where you describe the events of a two-month journey, complete with the day-to-day life on-board, and the tasks of the crew. Look up some specialized reading material to help you with the information.

A Visit of the Intendant.

(*L. R. Batchelor.*)

By kind permission of the Dominion Archives, Ottawa.

The Peopling of the Colony

The population of the colony continued to grow in spite of the dangers posed by those long and arduous ocean crossings. The census which I had taken just after my arrival showed 763 people employed in various trades. You must add to this the wives and children of these people, as well as the farmers and their families, and of course, the soldiers who decided to stay in New France. In 1660, the country had 2,500 inhabitants — and 6,500 in 1670! They tell me that 10 years later the population rose to 10,000.

I had always considered that the growth of the population was one of the essential cogs in the political machinery of the colony. The phrase "we can but live from day to day," which I heard from the inhabitants at that time, did not lie well with me. Very soon, I realized that one of the surest means of building the economy was to increase the rate of immigration. It was with this in mind that we had 1,500 immigrants landing in the colony between the years 1665 and 1672. Over and above that, we paid the passages of workers who had to stay three years in the colony with an established colonist. During this time they received a small recompense, and were happy to know that they too would have their own parcel of land at the end of their three-year stay. There were also those to whom we gave several arpents[*] of land already cleared and sown. The soldiers of the Carignan-Salières Regiment were encouraged to stay in the colony, and almost 1,000 filles du Roi arrived also. In 1671, 700 births were registered! All these facts I could proudly report to M. Colbert.

a)   If you had been the intendant of the colony, what would you have done to help increase the population? Write a report on this question.

b)   In a group, launch a publicity campaign to inform the French population of the seventeenth century of all that life in our colony had to offer. Use various means to make your campaign both striking and efficient, for example drawings, announcements, slogans, short articles and testimonials from the people already established in the colony.

---

[*] An arpent covered about one acre of land, or roughly 3,400m², as you say in your century. The arpent was the standard measure of land in our time, and is still used in Quebec and Louisiana in your day.

The Trades

Here is the distribution of the various *états* — trades or professions — between the years 1665 and 1666:

Trade		Trade	
Aiguiseur d'épées — sword sharpener	1	Fabricant de chandelles — candle-maker	3
Armurier — armourer	4	Ferblantier — tinsmith	1
Arquebusier — gunsmith	7	Fondeur — founder	1
Bailli — bailiff	4	Gentilhomme — nobleman	16
Bijoutier — jeweller	1	Imprimeur — printer	1
Boucher — butcher	7	Instituteur — teacher	3
Boulanger — baker	11	Jardinier — gardener	3
Brasseur — brewer	1	Maçon — mason	32
Briquetier — brick maker	1	Manchonnier — sleeve maker	1
Capitaine de navire — ship's captain	1	Marchand — shopkeeper	18
Chapelier — hatter	7	Matelot — sailor	32
Charpentier — carpenter	36	Menuisier — joiner	27
Charron — wheelwright	2	Meunier — miller	9
Chaudronnier — brazier	3	Notaire — notary	3
Chirurgien — surgeon	5	Sabotier — clog maker	1
Charbonnier — collier	1	Sellier — saddler	3
Cloutier — nail maker	4	Serrurier — locksmith	3
Confiseur — confectioner	5	Taillandier — edge-tool maker	14
Cordier — rope maker	6	Tailleur de pierre — stonecutter	1

Cordonnier — shoemaker	20	Tailleur — tailor	30
Corroyeur — currier	8	Tisserand — weaver	16
Coutelier — cutler	1	Tisserand de tapis — carpet weaver	3
Couvreur — roofer	1	Tonnelier — cooper	8
Domestique — servant	401	Tourneur — turner	1
Drapier — draper	4		
Fabricant de boutons — button maker	1	Total:	763

As you can guess, we encouraged France to send us people whose trades corresponded to our needs in the colony. For example, once the shipbuilding yards started up their activity, we appealed more and more to those carpenters specializing in keel making. We did the same with the surveyors, professionals skilled in the techniques of land measurement, as they were indispensable for the precise distribution of the land. Whenever there was a need, we appealed to the sense of duty and spirit of adventure of the French men and women.

a) Which profession or trade would you have chosen to follow if you had lived in the seventeenth century? (Consult a dictionary to find the meanings of any words you do not know: many of the trades mentioned in the list have disappeared from your century.) Have your friends in the group do the same. Discuss your respective choices.

b) Use the above list — where the trades are in alphabetical order — to make an illustrated glossary. Try to be precise in your drawings: take care in the drawing of tools, for example. You may find good illustrations in your library.

c) Soldier, farmer, baker, fisherman, administrator: find out about each of these five occupations as they would have been in the seventeenth century, and set up a comparison of them. You can keep in mind the following aspects: revenue or wages, way of life, place of residence, social status, tools or equipment used.

HENRY IV AND HIS FAMILY

The Fur Trade

The routine life of the villagers and farmers did not suit everyone. Between 1670 and 1672, there was an exodus of young Frenchmen from their homes and villages. These young people were thirsty for adventure; they became known as the coureurs de bois. The reason for such an exodus, in the majority of cases, was the attraction of the fur trade. (Sieur de Monts, the associate of Samuel de Champlain, had received the hunting and fur-trading monopoly from Henri IV, King of France.) So, these young people who had fled the quiet, simple life of the habitant travelled over hill and dale, across woods and forests, up and down rivers, braving all kinds of dangers to find the Native people with whom they could trade. Quite often, they were away for a year or perhaps two, only to return to their departure point — Québec or Ville-Marie — their simple birchbark canoes laden with rich furs. In exchange, the merchants would pay them in money or merchandise. True enough it was a job, a decent way of doing business, but the way of life of these young and bold coureurs de bois did not please everyone. As for me, in my position of authority in New France, I wanted to encourage the expansion of the fur trade, naturally, but I did not want to give unbridled freedom to these young, audacious fellows.

a) Let us show proof of *our* courage and imagination now! Do you think the colony of New France would have been as prosperous as it was (at least for the merchants) without the fur trade? Do you believe it could have existed without this flourishing commerce? Give your answer to these questions in writing; do not hesitate to say what you really think.

b) In a group, prepare a scene from the history of the fur trade. You will have two coureurs de bois, two fur merchants and two Native people; do not forget our powerful governor who followed this profitable trade very closely. The setting is a trade fair in Montréal, now an important commercial centre. The bartering begins — furs for all kinds of merchandise — and excitement fills the air! You remember of course that our governor smokes the peace pipe to open the fair. Use this element in your skit.

François de Laval
The King's Bishop

Le Conseil souverain — The Sovereign Council

Here is the organizational chart showing the administration of New France in the seventeenth century:

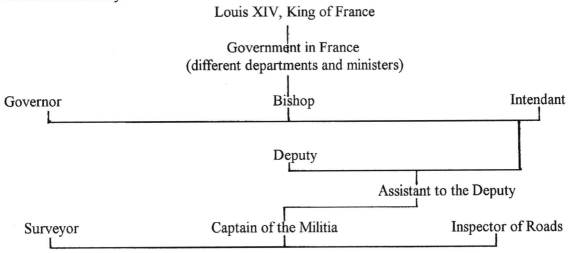

Louis XIV, King of France

Government in France
(different departments and ministers)

Governor   Bishop   Intendant

Deputy

Assistant to the Deputy

Surveyor   Captain of the Militia   Inspector of Roads

The forming of the Sovereign Council in the April of 1663 marked the establishing of the royal judiciary system in New France. Composed of the Governor, the Bishop and the Intendant (myself), and five councillors (usually seigneurs), this Council was the highest law-making body in the land. It was we three — the Governor, the Bishop and myself — who had to choose the councillors.

On January 24, 1667, I announced publicly my intention to re-establish law and order in the colony. I was told later that the laws drawn up by the Sovereign Council during my term in office were coherent and realistic; that pleased me.

a)   The meeting chamber of the Sovereign Council is a large hall in a building in the town of Québec. Imagine you are there, seated at the big table. Recreate a council meeting with your group: do not forget that the Governor, the Bishop, the five councillors and myself are all present. We discuss various topics — you add to the discussion — with regard to the administration of the colony. Let each person state his or her opinion!

b)   How would you have changed the administrative organization of the colony? Write a report for M. Colbert's eyes only — so it is open and frank, hiding none of the difficulties you are certainly going to meet. The report might have met with opposition from the influential people in New France. Show some boldness and imagination in your proposals.

c)   Examine closely the diagram of the administration of New France. I know that there are many ways of governing a country in your century. Choose three countries and study their administrative systems. Draw a diagram showing the distribution of powers in each of these countries. Compare the four systems. What are the advantages and disadvantages of each one?

Portrait of a seventeenth century Frenchman bearing arms

Le capitaine de milice — *The Captain of the Militia*

You read "Captain of the Militia" in the diagram of the administration of New France. The captain was usually a farmer who was placed at the head of a little troop of soldiers, all volunteers. This post required strong character, courage and initiative. Apart from his military responsibilities, the captain had other jobs: he ensured there was a liaison between the intendant, the ordinary people and the seigneurs. So, for example, when any work that was in the public interest had to be carried out, it was the captain who issued the order to whichever seigneur was responsible for it.

a)   The militia comprised a corps of volunteers who reinforced a very weak army in New France. In your time, a volunteer police force is often called a militia. Choose between these two occupations: a professional soldier — an *engagé* — or a farmer who belongs to the local militia. Write down the reasons for your choice.

b)   As the captain of the Militia — the *capitaine de milice* — you are going to launch a powerful recruitment campaign to attract men to your troop of volunteers. With a few friends, draw posters and write slogans to convince the men in the area to join your corps. Do not forget to emphasize the benefits of being a *milicien*.

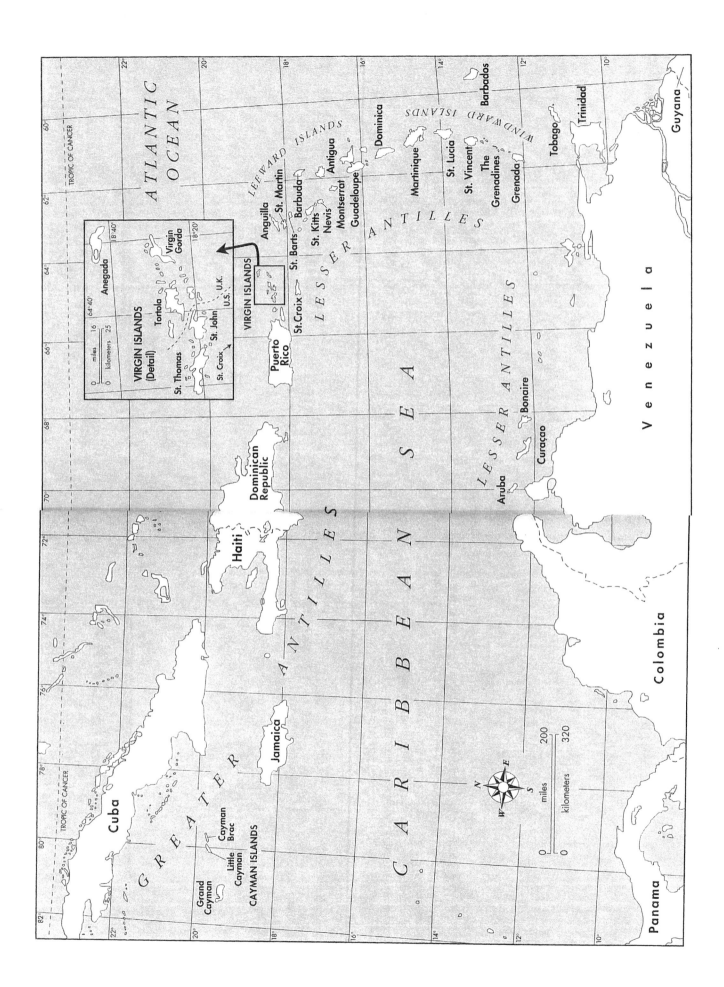

The West India Company*

We could not see the advantage of having a commercial company continue to run the colony. The colonists were not showing the enthusiasm for the company — the *Compagnie des Cent Associés* — that they had shown previously. The Company, founded by Cardinal Richelieu, had had the sole right to own property in New France for many a year. Now it seemed no longer up to the task. The colonists demanded an end to its rights, and Louis XIV agreed in 1663: New France became once more a *royal* possession.

One year later, however, the King set up a new company called the West India Company — the *Compagnie des Indes occidentales*. He granted it all rights of seigneury, property and justice. However, he reserved for himself the privilege of choosing and naming the governor and the councillors of the Sovereign Council.

In 1666, the Company named a lieutenant general to oversee the criminal and civil trials in Québec; in the same year, the town of Trois-Rivières saw the establishment of its first court of justice. In 1667, ships from the Company transported the first cargo of wood, peas, fish and seal oil from New France to West India. These same ships then headed for France laden with sugar from West India. Such a three-way commerce was at the very heart of the plan I myself had conceived. However, right from the start, my relationship with the Company had been rather difficult. I saw that it ran too often against the interests of the colony, odd as that might seem. As the Company had its grip firmly on all the commerce and navigation, it paralyzed any initiative taken by the colonists. Because of this poor state of affairs, the administrative and law-making systems had to try to take away some of its rights and privileges — gradually, of course.

I had many animated discussions with M. Colbert, where I let it be known that the Company was in fact hindering the growth of the colony. It was the King who decided to reinstate free trade in 1666. Thanks to this act, any merchant, be he a member of the Company or not, could ply his trade to the very best of his ability. Three years later, the King decided to free commerce even further — and the law he passed then had a very long life.

a) In your opinion, is a monopoly a good thing? From what point of view? Draw up a list of the advantages and disadvantages of the existence of a monopoly in a colony which has just been founded.

b) You are one of the administrators of the West India Company. You and I are discussing the present (seventeenth century) situation in the colony: the development of commerce, the centralization of power, the feelings of distrust that I have towards the Company. With a friend, present this interview to the class.

c) Write a letter to a business or a society of your century. You are interested in its aims, administrative structure, operations, social benefits, and the good it does for the community or the country. Make your questions pertinent and polite.

---

* You refer to West India as the Greater and Lesser Antilles, most of the islands in the West Indies.

The arrival of filles du Roi in the colony

Les filles du Roi — Daughters of the King

One very bold plan that turned out to be most fruitful was one which Louis XIV, M. Colbert and I had made. The plan was to send a number of young unmarried women — aged between 16 and 40 — to New France. We called them filles du Roi because they were without relatives and had been raised by the State, and so had the King for a father. He could take charge of their future as fathers did at that time for their daughters.

In the beginning, I did not approve of the choice of people who had been sent to us, because there were 12-year-olds and beggars among them. I asked M. Colbert to accept only people who were in good mental and physical condition, and also to choose from all social classes. Sometimes a dowry was given to the very poor among them. After a difficult two-month crossing, these filles du Roi disembarked at Québec, where they were welcomed by religious women, administrators, and a whole crowd of men impatient to find themselves a partner.

Almost 1,000 young women arrived in New France between 1665 and 1673 as part of this project. In 1670, I could write to M. Colbert saying that every woman who had arrived the previous year was already a mother. It is true that we put pressure on the young men who remained single: if they persisted in their unmarried state, we taxed them, and forbade them fishing, hunting and fur-trading rights. We had to have the means to achieve our end, you see. On the other side of the coin, the couples who had 10 children or more received a gift of money and were even granted certain privileges. All in all it was a great success; Louis XIV and his minister could be as proud of it as I was!

a) You are a fille du Roi. One week has passed since you arrived in Québec. You are writing the first page of your personal diary, describing what you have seen and heard in New France during this hectic week.

b) Draw up a list of qualities — mental, physical, emotional and spiritual — which you think the filles du Roi had to have if they were going to have any chance of success and happiness in New France. You can also say what you think of the categories already proposed in my time: *Petiz et grans et beaulz et laidx.*

c) And now, to the theatre! In a group, create a little play (comedy or tragedy according to your taste) which will depict the arrival of a ship carrying filles du Roi. The wharf is swarming with people. There is hustle and bustle all around. Questions are asked, shouts are heard, excitement is everywhere. Discuss the dialogue beforehand, choose a dramatic director, an artistic director and several actors. Do not forget to make some props and even some scene sets. Now on with the show!

Jean Talon at the first shipyard in New France

The Industries

To my way of thinking, commerce between New France, France and West India was a fundamental element of our development. The busy wharves where the seigneurs, habitants, administrators and merchants came together were a sign of the growing prosperity of the colony. Looking at the economic situation, I decided that if we could create industries based on the natural resources of the country, we could meet the needs of the population. We could start exporting much more. We would then have not only a subsistence economy, but the beginning of a profitable export trade.

And so I found myself gazing at our immense forests and abundant rivers, and thinking that here was an industry right under our noses: we had wood and the means to transport it! I thought I would use this wood for shipbuilding. I encouraged the growing of hemp and flax for the rope making and weaving industries respectively. I also encouraged the planting of hops and barley, which I bought for my brewery — one of my biggest successes! The manufacture of hats and shoes was going well also, the first thanks to the beaver pelts, and the second to the tannery at Pointe-Lévis.

My dream of a large fishing industry came to pass after my return to France. That project joined all the others I had started. The colony as a whole was becoming more and more prosperous. Alas, most of these industries, even the brewery which had gone so well, hardly survived my departure.

a) Choose one of the industries mentioned above and gather information about it with a friend. Both of you can make a mini-project which will include drawings, diagrams and reports based on the state of this industry in your century.

b) Design a series of postage stamps that will represent the various industries of New France at the start of its growth. Send your completed set to Canada Post. (I believe that is what you call the service in your time.)

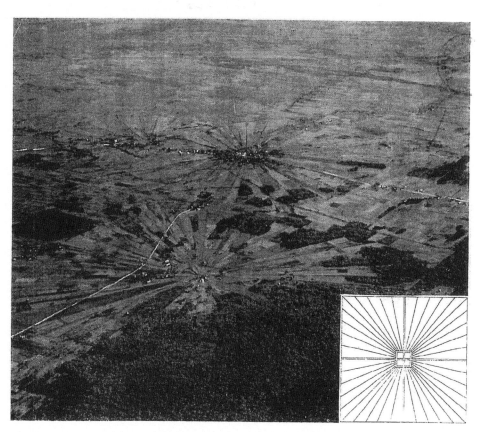

CHARLESBOURG

An aerial photograph of Charlesbourg, taken in 1936, shows the layout of the land much as it was in the latter half of the seventeenth century

The Farms

One of my favourite ideas was the establishment of communities of farmers. I had founded three quite close to the town: Bourg-Royal, Bourg-la-Reine and Bourg-Talon. To help make this idea work, the Jesuits — whom M. Colbert knew how to convince in his usual firm manner — agreed to give me a part of their land, the Seigneury of Notre-Dame-des-Anges. The plan of each community was a triangle, and each one was built around a site reserved for a church. Accordingly, people lived very near to one another: near their neighbours, the priest, the surgeon and the notary. Thanks to these communities, I could prepare in good time the 30 or 40 pieces of land that M. Colbert wanted each year for the new families settling in New France.

a) Peas, beans, corn, hops, flax and hemp were the main produce cultivated on these farms. Compare these crops with what is grown on the farms of your time, in your country, in your region. What similarities and what differences can you see? Imagine you are a reporter with the magazine *Agriculture in Our Region*, for which you are writing an article on this comparison.

b) You are a farmer in the community of Bourg-Talon, surrounded by your neighbours. One of your friends, on the other hand, is an habitant who stays in a seigneury on the bank of the river, quite far away from the other farmers. Make up a dialogue showing the advantages and disadvantages of living where you do, in your different environments. Rehearse this little dialogue and, when it is ready, present it to the class.

c) What kinds of animals were to be found on the farms of New France in my era, that is to say the third quarter of the seventeenth century? Make a list (which you can illustrate with pictures and reproductions of paintings of the time, for example) and beside each animal, mention the benefits we received from it.

It was my great pleasure to talk to you. I wish you a very fine good day! Adieu!

Jean Talon

Magdelaine de Verchères

La Seigneurie de Verchères,
le 3 septembre 1693

Bonjour, my dear Friend,

My name is Marie-Magdelaine Jarret de Verchères. Let me tell you my story and, first of all, the historical facts behind it. The wars in the colony will become part of your daily life; you will get used to living in my home, a little fort surrounded by a palisade. We shall hear the resounding boom of the cannons, the echoing shouts of the Iroquois, and the splashing of oars in the river. Always on the lookout, we shall learn the meaning of danger and fear; and we shall never forget our supreme duty to God and king. Believe me, my dear friend, when I say that I await your arrival impatiently.

Marie-Magdelaine Jarret de Verchères

Magdelaine de Verchères
1678 - 1747

Hello, my dear friend. I have a story from my past to tell you, a story that goes back to the *petite guerre*. Who knows, maybe one day a similar event will happen to you, and it will take a lot of your courage to see it through.

My name is Marie-Magdelaine Jarret de Verchères. That might sound like an odd name to you, but in the year of grace 1678 a simple Marie Jarret would not have done, you see, because my father, François Jarret, and my mother, Marie Perrot, owned the Seigneury of Verchères. I was born on March 3, 1678, in the manor house at Verchères on the south shore of our beautiful St. Lawrence River.

I was the fourth child of twelve — yes, that's right, twelve children — and I was without a doubt the boldest in the family. I loved adventure and I was always ready to face danger: there certainly was that back then.

The Native peoples travelled all over the area; after all, it was their land. It was the Iroquois who lived in our vicinity. Our presence was a threat to them. They came up the Richelieu River, the *rivière des Iroquois*, their main access to our fields. I say *our* fields; in their eyes they came to reclaim what was *their* land, *their* heritage. They came in their canoes, handling them skillfully and boldly. They came to face *us*, who had to repel them using our own brand of skill and audacity.

I remember one of those fresh, sunny days in October, one of many such days in autumn. It was in 1692 if I remember correctly. I was just 14, and I was walking along the riverbank. Imagine you are there beside me; you can be part of my story. You feel the autumn wind in your face and you see the grey water at your feet. The baskets of washing are set down on the bank; everything is quiet and peaceful. I remember that I was in charge of the seigneury that morning, young as I was, because my father was in Québec and my mother was in Montréal. My two older brothers, Antoine and François-Michel, had been taken by the Iroquois. I felt that the safety of the seigneury depended on me.

Look over there at the fields where my father's tenants are working; it's hard work. The land is fertile here and there is water; all the same, life is difficult, especially with the harsh winters. The tall, baldheaded tenant is Robert Taillefer. There are 15 in his little house, would you believe it?

Wait a moment.... What's that I hear? A musket shot? There's another one! There they are — the Iroquois — I see them; they're taking Monsieur Taillefer! Quick! Run back to the house! Keep to the path, I'm coming, I'm coming. Oh no, there's one! He has me, he has my fichu, I can't get away. If I can just undo the knot on the fichu — there, it's undone! I'm coming. Run, through the gates of the fort — inside, inside! Help me push them shut and bar them! Done! Now I think we're safe; we must come up with a plan.

"Gather round, everyone here in the fort. Stop what you're doing and listen to me!

Outside the palisade right now there are 30 or 40 Iroquois; here there are just seven of us. We have to make them believe there are more of us. You men have to take to the palisade, firing here and there and changing position as much as you can; you women help with the guns. Give me a man's hat and a musket, and I'll fire too! Don't stop firing for a moment, or they'll think there aren't many people in here."

You stay with me, my friend, you're not used to this. With a little luck, our cannons will be heard along the river, and other forts might come to our aid. This day is either going to be very long — or extremely short.

Dusk crept quietly across the land, and night began to fall. Not a sound. I knew the Iroquois had already taken about 20 prisoners outside the palisade. They would go back now, as was their custom. Next morning, right enough, they had all gone, and the Chevalier de Crizafi arrived from Montréal with 100 of his militia. They had heard our cannons and had set out by canoe. And 50 Native friends had also rushed to our aid — on foot! The fort had been saved, and we had saved it! I became a heroine of New France, and I was only 14! They say a legend was born that day, a legend about a girl who was full of courage and resourcefulness. That was me, with your help of course.

And what became of this bold little lass? Well, my father died, and I stayed on at the fort to look after my mother, and also to see to the business side of things. I married Pierre-Thomas Tarieu de la Pérade in 1706. I was 28, which was quite old to marry at that time, compared to my mother, for example, who was 12 when she married.

I left Verchères for the Seigneury of Sainte-Anne de la Pérade. And what was life like there? They say in the history books that I became rather a bossy person, and that I always had to have the last word. Oh well, too bad, you'll always find nasty tongues wherever you go.

I died on August 8, 1747; I was 69. It is said there were many priests at my funeral. In this way, New France paid me homage and awarded me a great honour.

A typical seigneurial fort
Fort Remy, Lachine, 1671

From Girouard's "Le Vieux Lachine"
1 Mill   2 Priest's House   3 Chapel
4 La Salle's House   5 Barn
6 Palisades   7 Bastions

The Seigneury

Just as your environment affects your life in your century, my friend, so did mine influence my life in the seventeenth century. The seigneury, the land controlled by the seigneur, was the foundation of the colonists' life in New France. The commission which the Marquis de la Roche headed in 1598 was formed precisely to create seigneuries, fiefdoms and baronies. The feudal system had been imposed on the colony by its mother country, France, where it was the result of many historical and social forces, my father told me.

As for us, we were in a new country here, a country where the climate was harsh and where the crop growing seasons were short — life was difficult. Our seigneurs were most often *not* of noble birth (which didn't prevent them from getting along with the king, the Sovereign Council and the intendant), but which did make a difference. For us, there was always the presence of hardship and danger. How was this seigneurial type of system going to work in New France? Life was quite different here from life in France.

a) Find out information about the feudal systems in France and its neighbouring countries. Compare them to that practised in New France, using two columns headed: similarities, differences.

b) Imagine you have the ear of an attentive king of France (that means he listens favourably to many of your suggestions — maybe not to all of them). You have certain ideas to propose about the organization of our little population in New France. You want to provide the colony with a stable and beneficial constitution. So, you write a report containing suggestions that would replace the feudal system with something more appropriate to our conditions here. Remember you are addressing the king, and as such he has his own fixed ideas on the question. Be courteous, creative and to the point!

c) Make a maquette or a plan of a seventeenth century seigneury. Include the boundaries of the land owned by the seigneur, the manor house itself, the palisade, the entrance gate, the bastions, the cultivated fields surrounding the fort, the cleared land beyond its boundaries and — most important of all — the river. Be accurate: this plan could represent the *domaine des Jarret*, our seigneury.

This life, regulated as it was by the seigneurial system, was my life, because I was a seigneur's daughter. You are now going to become my brother or sister, because in this way you can share my daily joys and sorrows. You will then be influenced by my environment, which is continually evolving, and you will change your way of life for mine — at least for a little while! So, come home with me....

Marius Barbeau

Dr. Marius Barbeau transcribing a recorded melody.

Music

There is a song I like — "Ah! Toi, belle hirondelle" — that is meant to be sung by a girl about my age, 14 or so. The song addresses its words to a bird, a swallow that is flying back and forth over land and water, looking for the girl's loved one who has left on his boat. The bird catches sight of Alexis, the beloved one, who is as sad as the girl, but who takes heart when the swallow gives him good news of her.

a) In a group, listen to this seventeenth century song from France if you can find a copy on a folk song cassette (I hear you have such things now).* Try to sing it yourself — it's not too difficult. If you play a musical instrument, try it on that too!

b) Create a cartoon based on the facts given in this most gentle song my mother used to sing to me. In a group of four, choose two artists and two scriptwriters. Treat each verse of the song with care and good taste, and try to have your text and drawings maintain the mood of the original work.

c) You are a composer. Write a simple melody on a subject that interests you. As for me, I would choose the river because it's always with me no matter what the season. Record your song and give it to someone you like as a present.

---

* There were to be several versions of this folk song in the well-known collections of (Charles) Marius Barbeau who was to live from 1883-1969. He was to become a renowned folklorist, studying Native and Quebec legends and folk songs. You will find one such version on the following pages. Sing it for me.

Ah! Toi, belle Hirondelle
(Swallow, Messenger of Love)

Collected by Marius Barbeau
English translation by
J. Murray Gibbon

Arranged by
Oscar O'Brien

1."Ah! toi, belle hi - ron - del - le, qui vole i - ci, N'as - tu pas vu dans ces î - les mon A - le - xis Qui est par - ti dans les voy -

1."Ah! thou so love - ly swallow, fly - ing up here, Have you seen round in these is - lands A - lex - is dear? He went a - way, he went a -

a - ges en ces longs jours? Il te don - ne - ra des nou -
voyag-ing long his so-journ, He'll make you sure kind - li - est

vel - les de son re - tour."
messen-ger of his re - turn!

2. L'oiseau qu'est tout aimable s'est envolé.
Avec son léger plumage s'en est allé
A traversé l'eau et la mer sans se lasser;
Dessus les mats de cette flotte s'est reposé.

3. A-t aperfu la hune d'un bâtiment.
Alexis s'y lamente en naviguant.
"Parle-moi donc, amant fidèle, parle-moi donc!
Je viens de la part de ta belle, dans ces vallons."

4. L'amant plein de surprise d'entendr' parler
De savoir des nouvelles d'sa bien-aimé':
"Tu lui diras, belle hirondelle, qu'à mes amours
Je lui serai chaste et fidèle à mon retour."

2. *The bird who is so friendly has flown away*
All afloat light on his feathers wafted away,
Across the sea over the ocean nor ever stay'd:
Till on the masts of a flotilla rest there he made.

3. *And there noticed a vessel with high topsail;*
Alexis was lamenting there at the wheel;
"Speak to me then, O faithful lover, speak to me then,
I am an envoy of the fair one across the main,"

4. *The swain now all astounded when this was said,*
To obtain so strange a message of his fair maid,
"O say to her, my lovely swallow as I have sworn,
I shall to him stay chaste and faithful till I return!"

Governor Frontenac with the British envoy who is demanding the surrender of Québec.

La petite guerre — The Little War

Songs usually accompanied those long, exhausting marches that the army undertook during the *petite guerre*. An odd sort of war, right enough! It was made up of three expeditions launched by the rather arrogant governor of the colony, Louis de Buade, Comte de Frontenac et de Palluau. These expeditions were launched against the English strongholds in New England. At that time, we were trying to protect ourselves from English skirmishes: in the Governor's eyes, the best form of defence was attack.

a)   Strange indeed is the phrase *petite guerre*. In my opinion, no war is ever small if it entails death or injury (without counting the violence committed against women and children, the pillaging, the destruction of harvests). But it is this peculiar name that history has given it. Your century is well acquainted with war; I know, because war is, alas, universal and timeless. Do you know of places where you could apply the term *petite guerre*? Draw up a list of them using the following headings: country or people; civil war or external conflict, causes, allies, length of conflict, possible solution. Think long and hard about this important question: it's necessary to know what is going on in your world.

b)   You are a journalist who is covering (as you say in the profession) the campaigns carried out by Comte de Frontenac in New England. You have to write an article and send it to the French press office to try to explain the actual situation to the French people. Remember that the pen can be mightier than the sword. Your article will be read all over France: weigh your thoughts well.

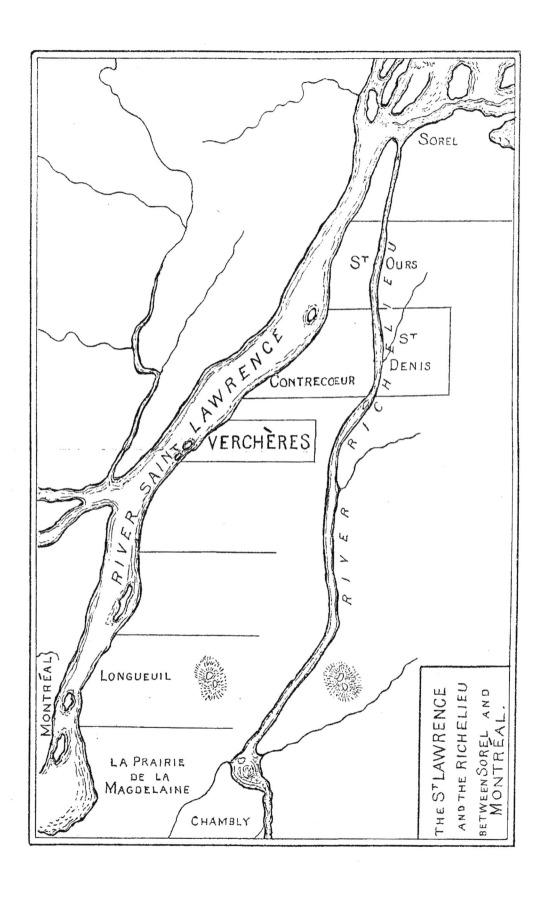

SOREL

ST OURS

ST DENIS

CONTRECŒUR

RIVER SAINT LAWRENCE

VERCHÈRES

RIVER RICHELIEU

MONTRÉAL

LONGUEUIL

LA PRAIRIE
DE LA
MAGDELAINE

CHAMBLY

THE ST LAWRENCE
AND THE RICHELIEU
BETWEEN SOREL AND
MONTRÉAL.

My Father, François Jarret, Sieur de Verchères

My father, Sieur de Verchères, for whom a military life meant everything, had arrived from France with his regiment — Prince Carignan's. When the majority of the troops from the Carignan-Salières Regiment were sent back in 1668, my father was one of a number of officers and soldiers who accepted the offer of lands beside the St. Lawrence River. My father settled on Île d'Orléans — lucky, wasn't he, to live on an island? There he married Marie Perrot, who was 12 years of age. In 1672 he received the concession of a seigneury of two and a half square miles* between Montréal and Sorel. He added other lands to it, and so was born the Seigneury of Verchères, situated between forts Chambly and Richelieu. François Jarret was respected by everyone, both as a former military man and as a seigneur.

a) Take on the role of my father. You are seated at the big table in the manor house surrounded by your family. Dinner is served, and someone asks you to tell one of your stories about your former military profession. Silence falls around the table, and you begin. Write your story, practise it aloud, and seated in a comfortable chair, surrounded by your friends, excite and charm them with what you relate from the past.

b) My father took care of the cultivation of his fields around the manor house. This occupation brought many worries and difficulties. Can you draw up a list of the obstacles he might have met, and suggest the ways in which he might have overcome each one? You'll be doing us a great service.

c) Find out what sort of produce we could have grown on our land. Do a mini-project on the subject, with drawings, pictures, diagrams and collages.

---

* This area would cover about six and a half square kilometres, as you say in your time. We called it a *lieue carrée*.

An elaborate French coat of arms

The Seigneur

The seigneur found out that it wasn't easy to make a living in New France. Of course there was produce he could grow to feed his people, but trade with the Native peoples, and the fur trade itself were forbidden to him. Even if he were treated as the master, the seigneur in our colony was only a pale shadow of the noble in France. The French nobility had been well entrenched on its lands for several generations.

However, the seigneur did enjoy some privileges: he could be given additional titles by the king; he could receive more land from the king; his tenants had to render fealty and homage to him, and pay him rent plus a fixed amount named *cens*. He also had some judiciary powers. In return, he had to render fealty and homage to the State — to the governor who represented the king. Also, he had to take an *aveu*, which is a written declaration by the seigneur stating the duty of each vassal to him. In addition, the seigneur had to inform the State of the exact number of people living at the seigneury, and the number of fields he possessed.

a) You are an interviewer who is questioning a young seigneur who has just arrived in the colony. Create an appropriate type of dialogue, taking into account the advantages and disadvantages the seigneur would have in such a situation.

b) Write up a contract between the seigneur and the habitant showing all their obligations one to the other. You can find useful information in your library about feudal systems in various countries.

c) Would you like to have been a seigneur, my friend? Me, too! Design your own coat of arms. The individual parts of the shield — and the colours — must represent your interests and your way of life as a seigneur.

Tav. 30 - ANTONIO CIFRONDI (1657-1730)
La cucitrice - The seamstress - Die Näherin - La couseuse
(Brescia, Galleria d'Arte Moderna)

My Mother, Marie Perrot

If I had had to design a coat of arms for my mother, I would have chosen courage as its theme. In fact, Marie Perrot was only 12 when my father, a lively young soldier, fell in love with her and married her. Their union was a fruitful one, as she had 12 children — an average-sized family at that time, I have to say. As you already know, our seigneury was in a dangerous area, as it was situated on the St. Lawrence River between Montréal and Sorel, quite near the Richelieu River, the *rivière des Iroquois*.

During the year 1690 danger was lurking nearby. One day our little fort of Verchères was attacked. It was my mother, a woman of audacious spirit and strong will, who saved us all. I have never forgotten that day when we succeeded in repelling the Iroquois. I can also remember the two long days which followed, as we awaited the arrival of the army. It was in the May of that same year that my brother, alas, died in a skirmish at Prairie de la Magdelaine.

a)   You are preparing for a television program in which you will be relating these events (they tell me that such inventions exist in your time). Write an objective and precise account, practise it and present it to the class. My mother would have been proud of you!

b)   You can imagine the role played by my mother in our family, she being the wife of a seigneur of the seventeenth century. It's likely that this type of role has changed greatly over the years. State the differences and similarities that you think exist between *her* role and that of a spirited, courageous woman of your century (as she was for hers).

c)   In a group, create a series of *tableaux vivants*. These are still, silent poses that you and your friends will adopt to depict the different types of tasks and chores that could have been my mother's duties. Have a narrator relate each scene.

ABOVE: "Ho Nee Yeath Taw No Row is depicted clasping a bow, suggesting that he is as ferocious and deadly a hunter as his fellow kings, but one who prefers to hunt by stealth. Although Verelst's portraits evidently seemed similar to him, each king resembling the others, the artist clearly attempted to introduce as many individual touches as possible to each canvas."

ABOVE: "Tee Yee Neen Ho Ga Row, emperor of the Five Nations Confederacy, was deemed superior to the other kings and is thus portrayed with a wampum belt, a sign among the Indians of supreme statesmanship and authority to negotiate as head chieftain. The crosses on the belt represent the League of Iroquois Nations. His black costume further denotes the leader in the delegation of leaders."

The Iroquois

We, the *Français*, felt the existence of the colony was threatened by the Iroquois, the Native people of the area. They no doubt felt the same about us. The French population of New France had to face up to almost daily dangers. These Native people had a good sense of the use of strategy, and they were well acquainted with our strengths and weaknesses. They hoped for two things, to break our courage and to dry up the source of our commerce. It was impossible to attack them head on en masse, because they just disappeared into the forests which they knew much better than we did of course (this was *their* land, after all!), and because they attacked only in little groups. Add to that the fact that the English were giving them some very useful help. Really, New France could have been wiped off the map easily, with hardly a trace to say it had been there....

a)   It has been said that the "Iroquois were fighting to defend their way of life and their lives, so much did they love freedom and hate constraint." What do you think about that? Prepare a debate on the subject. Choose a friend who thinks as you do and two others who oppose your view. Be as just as you can, and try to understand the real and profound reasons for the hostility of the Iroquois in this regard.

b)   Do some research on other countries where a similar situation has arisen, that is where the indigenous peoples have fought against strangers who came to conquer their lands or to "pacify" them, or both. Who has won in most cases, if not all? Who has lost legitimate rights? Draw up a list of these conquests and colonial wars using the following headings: native people's country, colonists' original homeland, length of the conflict, result.

c)   Learn about the Iroquois. The library can offer you exciting works about them. Make a mini-project out of this research, using maps, drawings and designs. Write a text after you have made a detailed plan, giving a title to each section.

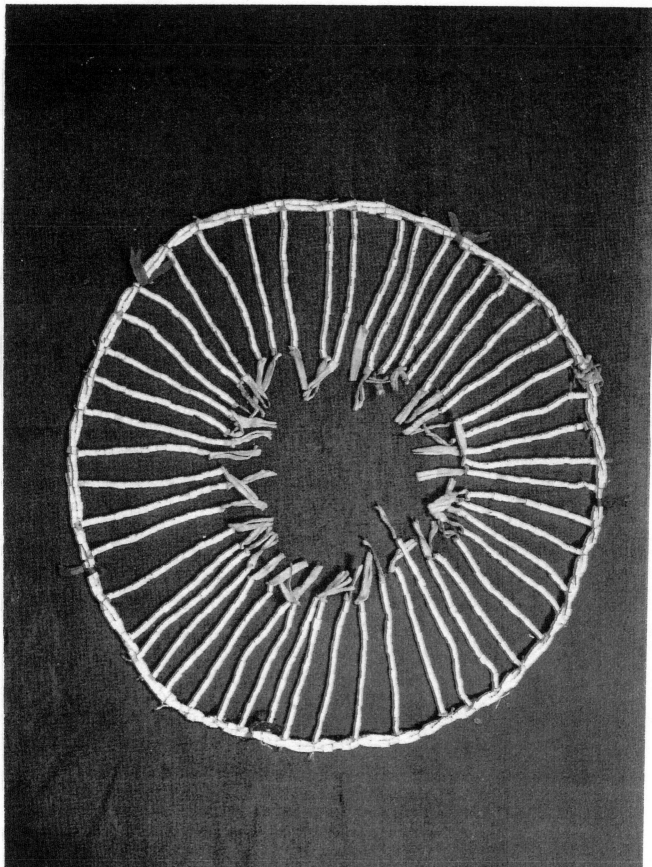

Wampum symbol of the Covenant of the League of the Five Nations

The League of the Five Nations

The Iroquois League, comprising five nations — the Cayuga, Mohawk, Seneca, Oneida and Onondaga — was formed by a peaceful, far-sighted Huron, Dekanawida, born in the mid-1400s near what you call Kingston, Ontario. This League was a fine democracy that had existed for years before we French came to colonize the land. The Tuscarora nation was to join it later. Some say this democracy was to be used in later years as a model by a huge country when writing its constitution. That country was going to be a union of states rather than nations. The League members had freedom of speech, freedom of belief and the right to hunt on one another's lands. Women were highly regarded and may have had the right to vote with the men. All in all, Dekanawida was an innovative thinker who produced excellent results.

a)   Assume that you are Dekanawida. You have a novel concept for your people to enable them to live a better and more peaceful life. In a group, prepare and deliver a speech in which you try to persuade the five nations to embrace your idea. The other members of the group may ask pertinent and pointed questions.

b)   In the library you will find information on democracies that have existed throughout the centuries. Choose five of those and classify them under the headings: founder(s), reason for founding, country, dates, outcome.

c)   You are a composer. Write a folk song telling the story of Dekanawida and his Iroquois League of the Five Nations — still existing in your century as the League of the Six Nations. Record it and present it to a friend.

KONDIARONK, known by the French as "Le Rat", a Tionontati or Petun Huron chief was born in 1649 and died in August, 1701 at Montréal, Québec. After the dispersal of the Hurons by the southern Iroquois, the displaced tribes sought the protection of the French governor; and it was during the negotiations with Frontenac that Kondiaronk was first noticed. Noted for his ability to gain political advantage in council. Kondiaronk played an active role as a negotiator up until the day he died. His funeral was attended by Iroquois, Huron and Ottawa warriors as well as the French governor and his soldiers. He lies buried somewhere near or beneath Montréal's Place d'Armes.

KONDIARONK, surnommé "Le Rat" par les Français, chef des Tionontati ou des Hurons Petun est né en 1649 et mourut au mois d'août 1701 à Montréal, Québec. Après la dispersion des Hurons par les Iroquois du Sud, les tribus exilées recherchèrent la protection du gouverneur français; et ce fut au cours des négociations avec Frontenac que Kondiaronk se fit remarquer. Ayant été reconnu pour son habilité à gagner des avantages politiques au cours d'une réunion du Conseil, il joua un rôle actif comme négociateur jusqu'au dernier jour de sa vie. A ses funérailles assistèrent des guerriers Iroquois, Hurons et Outaouais aussi bien que le gouverneur français et ses soldats. Il fut enseveli quelque part auprès ou en dessous de la Place d'Armes à Montréal.

Le comte de Frontenac et de Palluau
1620-1698

Comte de Frontenac was sent back to New France in 1689 in the hope that he could conquer the Iroquois, or at least quell them into submission. His first term of office as governor, from 1672-1682, had made him popular with the population of the colony, but he had been recalled to France by the administration. He was an energetic and charming man, although arrogant and self-seeking. He was well acquainted with both life at court and life in the military establishment. He was often well received by the Native peoples, dancing with them, and enjoying their fellowship. In this way he hoped to influence them to the best of his ability.

However, the Iroquois didn't let themselves be seduced. Frontenac reinforced the fortifications in Québec, Montréal and Trois-Rivières. He asked France to send him 1,000 men. Henceforth, the army protected us as we worked in the fields, and that was good, but we continued to experience famine and all sorts of other difficulties. So, in spite of his boldness and youthful type of zeal, Governor Frontenac never really succeeded in containing the threat of the Iroquois.

a) I quite liked Comte de Frontenac, or what I knew about him at least. What would you have done in his place? Write a letter to Louis XIV, suggesting a policy or a strategy for improving the state of affairs in New France.

b) We know something about Comte de Frontenac's plans in New France. Choose one aspect that interests you, write an account of it, practise its narration, and tell it to the class. Accompany your story with music. Here you are, a storyteller.

c) Look closely at a portrait of Comte de Frontenac. His clothing lacks nothing in charm, does it? In fact, it's quite fancy! In your opinion, did he dress like that to impress the people around him? Name six people in your century who dressed or dress to create a certain effect on those around them. Perhaps they provoke admiration and respect, perhaps astonishment or even envy. Describe how they succeed in affecting people in this way, just by their dress. I shall read what you write with a great deal of interest because I have my favourite clothes too.

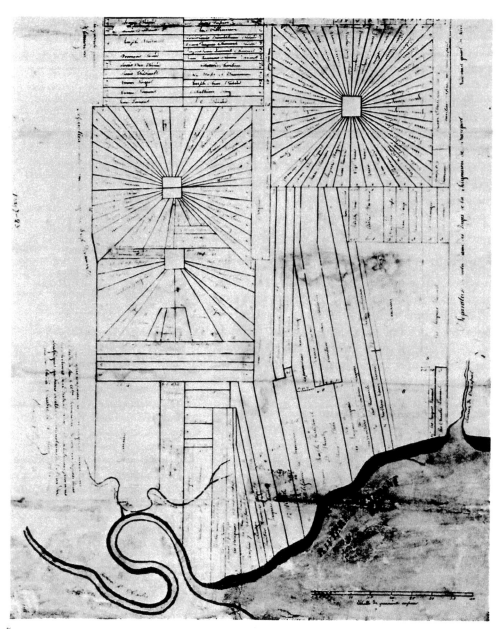

"Devised to foster a self-sufficient and stable agricultural society, the seigneurial method of
land tenure was a derivative of the feudal system transplanted in Canada in 1623. The map
shows the allotment of lands to censitaires (tenants) in the seigneuries of Charlesbourg and
Beauport near Québec City. The small squares at centre represent the landowners' manors."

The Seigneury of Verchères

The effect that the Seigneury of Verchères wanted to produce was one of security. All along the St. Lawrence River and also along the Richelieu River, there was intense activity: here, trees were being felled, there, stakes were being sunk to erect a palisade. Our manor house had already been surrounded by a palisade 14 feet high. Its entrance way faced the river. We had erected a bastion at each corner of the palisade, and in front of it we had left a large space, cleared, that allowed us to see anyone who was approaching. The fields stretched even farther out, and we cultivated some land inside our "walls" also. As for the manor house, it was big enough to lodge everyone, the homes, warehouses and barns all grouped around our main building. Everything was protected with the exception of the fields.

a) Look for reproductions of the forts and seigneuries of my time. From your research and from what I have told you, draw a plan or make a maquette of the Seigneury of Verchères. Don't forget the river: after all, our colony was founded on the St. Lawrence River.

b) You are one of the workers who is busy constructing the manor house and its surrounding buildings. As you know how to write, you must write a report to my father, in which you describe the progress being made in the construction, the difficulties you have encountered, and the finishing date. Remember to show respect by the tone of your letter.

c) Many years ago, particularly in the Middle Ages, entire towns were surrounded by ramparts, crenellated walls and towers. Enormous gates were opened and closed to allow and prevent access to the town. What advantages and disadvantages do you see in such a defence system? Draw up a list in two columns and compare it to your friends' lists.

salt	50 *sols* per *minot*
pepper	20 *sols* per *once*
chickens	1 *livre* each
geese	1 *livre* and 5 *sols* each
sheep	15 *livres* each
pigs	22 *livres* each
pewter dishes	15 *sols* each
gun shot	4 *livres* per thousand
nails	20 *livres* per thousand
glass beads	8 *sols* per *livre*
hand saws	18 *livres* 15 *sols* each
winter coats	3 *livres* each
ladies' shoes	100 *sols* each
iron pots	6 *livres* each
scissors	7 *sols* a pair
rosary beads	7 *sols* a string
olive oil	14 *sols* a pot
gun powder	30 *sols* a *horn*
guns	20 *livres* each

The Habitant

Our workers lived in little homes nestled around the manor house, and therefore protected by the wooden palisade. They had to pay the *cens* or "quitrent" to my father each year, and so they were called *censitaires*, or very often, habitants. They had certain obligations to my father. They had to clear the land, take care of sowing and reaping the harvests, and make the necessary preparations for the coming of winter (the cutting of trees and the gathering of wood, the storing of grain and seeds). When they worked in the fields, they were protected by the soldiers; one cannon shot announced the approach of the enemy.

Along with the *cens*, the habitants had to pay rent either in money or in produce. For example, if they had an arpent* of land, they had to pay 20 sols*, or one capon. The habitants also had to render fealty and homage to their seigneur. Taking everything into account, their life could have been worse: without a doubt it was much better than the one they had known in France before they came to the colony.

a) Imagine a group of habitants discussing their life at the Seigneury of Verchères. You and your friends take part in the discussion. Prepare the scene — which can be very lively — rehearse it and present it to the whole class.

b) My father, Sieur de Verchères, is busy writing a report to Governor Frontenac. He wants to give him an account of the number of his habitants, and he wants to stress the importance of the cultivation of his land. He will also confirm his *aveu*, which is a written acknowledgment of the duties of his vassals to him as seigneur, concerning the land he has given them. Compose this letter in a suitable style.

c) You are an habitant, one of the seigneur's workers, but you dream of becoming a coureur de bois. You imagine the adventures and fascinating life these young people lead; they have no ties, no master, and perhaps no faith to guide them and no law to restrain them. Write a poem with this theme. Choose a piece of music that could go with your flight of fancy. Present it to the class.

---

* This area would have covered about one acre, or roughly 3,400m², as you say in your day. The arpent was the standard measure of land in my time, and is still used in Quebec and Louisiana in your century.

* The sol, one of our coins, was made of either copper or silver, and was usually worth $\frac{1}{20}$ of a livre; a livre, my friend, was worth a pound of silver.

The Trades

Of course there were those who dreamt of *la folle aventure* (crazy adventure) that would lead them over hills and dales, through woods and forests, across lakes and rivers — to the end of the world! But there were also all the others who contented themselves with a quieter life, and perhaps a more productive one. The various trades in which they were engaged were indispensable to the survival and the continued flourishing of the colony. Here is a list of the trades and professions of the colonists in New France between the years 1665 and 1666:

Aiguiseur d'épées — sword sharpener	1	Fabricant de chandelles — candle-maker	3
Armurier — armourer	4	Ferblantier — tinsmith	1
Arquebusier — gunsmith	7	Fondeur — founder	1
Bailli — bailiff	4	Gentilhomme — nobleman	16
Bijoutier — jeweller	1	Imprimeur — printer	1
Boucher — butcher	7	Instituteur — teacher	3
Boulanger — baker	11	Jardinier — gardener	3
Brasseur — brewer	1	Maçon — mason	32
Briquetier — brick maker	1	Manchonnier — sleeve maker	1
Capitaine de navire — ship's captain	1	Marchand — shopkeeper	18
Chapelier — hatter	7	Matelot — sailor	32
Charpentier — carpenter	36	Menuisier — joiner	27
Charron — wheelwright	2	Meunier — miller	9
Chaudronnier — brazier	3	Notaire — notary	3
Chirurgien — surgeon	5	Sabotier — clog maker	1
Charbonnier — collier	1	Sellier — saddler	3
Cloutier — nail maker	4	Serrurier — locksmith	3

Confiseur — confectioner	5	Taillandier — edge-tool maker	14
Cordier — rope maker	6	Tailleur de pierre — stonecutter	1
Cordonnier — shoemaker	20	Tailleur — tailor	30
Corroyeur — currier	8	Tisserand — weaver	16
Coutelier — cutler	1	Tisserand de tapis — carpet weaver	3
Couvreur — roofer	1	Tonnelier — cooper	8
Domestique — servant	401	Tourneur — turner	1
Drapier — draper	4		
Fabricant de boutons — button maker	1	Total:	763

All the men hunted and fished, fishing especially for eel, which was abundant in the St. Lawrence River and which we salted for winter consumption. They all participated in felling the trees, as we needed wood for heating and for construction. Weaving was not widespread yet, and there was little fabric in the country. We were really badly dressed, in spite of some "presents" received from the Crown. On the other hand, a fine lifestyle could be seen in Québec, where the merchants found outlets for their fineries and knick-knacks. The town of Québec was a true capital, full of fun and quite fashion conscious.

a) Which occupation would *you* have chosen, out of all these listed here? (Consult a dictionary for the ones you don't know: several don't exist in your day.) Write a text stating the reasons for your choice. Before deciding, think about your talents and your hobbies.

b) Read the list of trades given above (they are in alphabetical order), and use it to make your own illustrated glossary. Make your drawings as simple and precise as possible (consult an old encyclopedia, where you'll find wonderful plates illustrating the various trades: for example, the famous *Grande Encyclopédie* that Diderot and his philosopher friends were about to write in the eighteenth century can be found in reproduction in many libraries.)

c) Many of the trades of the seventeenth century don't exist today, or have been replaced by others. Try to classify the trades in the list according to their capacity to last. Make three columns with headings: trades or professions of the seventeenth century only; trades or professions that have replaced the ones of the seventeenth century; trades or professions that have lasted almost 300 years.

CHORUS JIG

This jig was written by Turlough O'Carolan, born in 1670 in County Meath, Ireland.
He died in 1738 in County Leitrim.

Our Entertainment

Do not think, my friend, that life was nothing but a long succession of chores, trials and dangers. We had pastimes, too. We held on dearly to many of the customs of the old country, in particular the fêtes (saints' days, fairs, festivals). The first of May, for example, was a very special day for us. In front of the manor house, the habitants erected a pole (a tree of course) to which they attached ribbons. We all danced and sang around it, and enjoyed the hospitality offered by my father. The *Saint-Martin* was a little different, but it too was an excuse for merriment. That was the day when the habitants had to pay their rent, so, once all the business had been taken care of, they enjoyed my father's hospitality — and he knew how to be a host, royally! We always celebrated a good harvest too, and of course, weddings and births.

a)   What fête or celebration from your century do you like most, and why? Give a description of it in your diary. Don't forget to write about how you feel as well as what you do. Let the fête begin!

b)   Invent three games suitable for the children of the seventeenth century. Think about our environment, about the tasks that some of us — especially the girls — had to carry out during the day, and about any free time we had. Draw sketches with labels, planned outlines and diagrams. Use your imagination!

c)   Someone once shared this thought with me, and I must say I found it both interesting and profound: "We don't stop playing because we grow older; we grow older because we stop playing." What do you think about this idea? Discuss these words with your friends, and make sure that each person listens respectfully to the other.

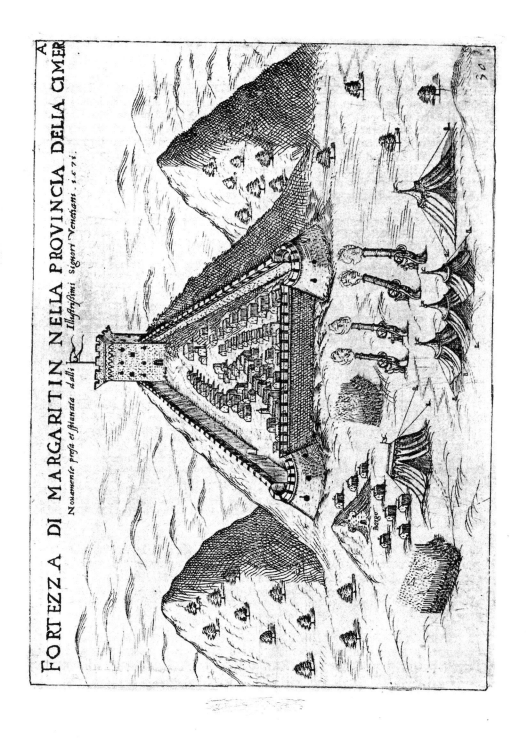

FORTEZZA DI MARGARTIN NELLA PROVINCIA DELLA CIMER

Nouamente presa et spianata dalli Illustrissimi Signori Venetiani. 1671.

Borgo

The Forts

Given that our survival was something that used a great deal of energy, it was only natural that forts played an essential role in our day-to-day existence. M. Prouville de Tracey, named as lieutenant-governor of Québec in 1665 by Louis XIV, built several important forts at strategic locations in the colony, for example those at Sorel and Chambly, in the area where we lived (named after the officers who were in command of them). If you lived near a fort you had the advantage of being protected; you also had access to a chapel and a mill.

a)   Find out about the forts constructed in my century — anywhere in the world. How do they differ from the ones built earlier and the ones built later? Make drawings, plans, diagrams and maps which will illustrate clearly these differences.

b)   Find several definitions of the French word *fort*. Think of other words, which we call homonyms and homographs, which can be used in various ways, for example *point, bas, canon, pique....* How many can you find?

c)   In a group of four, take on the roles of soldiers. You have been posted to Fort Chambly; you have just finished guard duty and you are sitting discussing your daily life, your duties, your pastimes (awaited with impatience), and the advantages and disadvantages the military profession has to offer. Be frank but polite with one another.

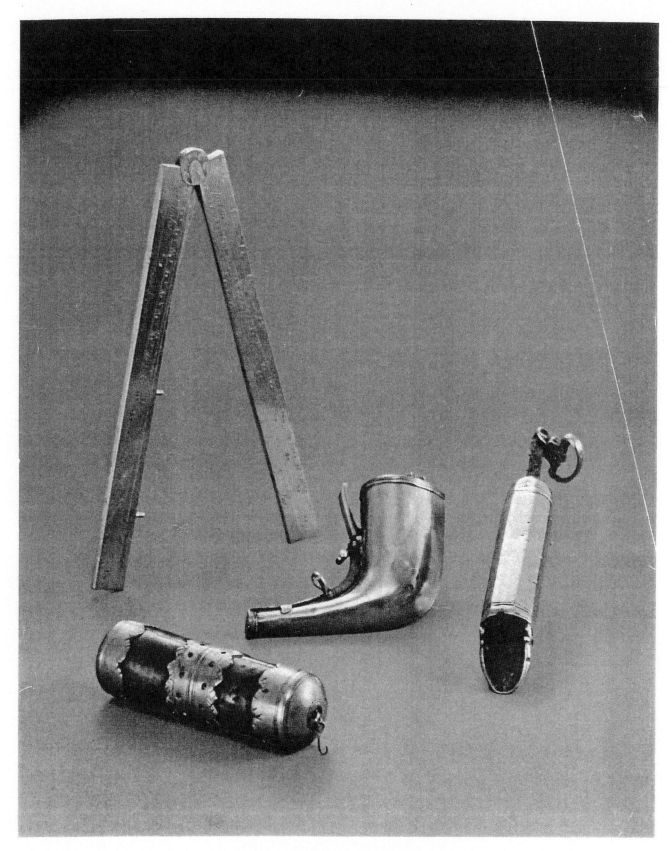

"An assortment of objects related to guns and gunpowder. The jointed rule is a seventeenth-century French artillerist's gauge and angle finder, as the inscriptions attest, designed to measure the caliber of firing weapons, the weight of the balls (*boulets*) to be propelled, and other data important to a cannoneer of the time. At the lower left is what may be a tinderbox, made of copper mounted in brass late in the seventeenth century. The two objects at the right are powder charges, both of Near Eastern origin and probably made in the eighteenth century."

The Weapons

It's not a big leap from soldiers to weapons, so we can make it easily. Each fort was provided with the usual artillery of the seventeenth century, cannons of every kind. Their noise frightened the enemy, and also warned the habitants of impending danger. Up to 1650, the musket, a portable weapon, had to be fired from a forked stand stuck into the ground. The halberd (a weapon with a long wooden handle having a sharp iron point and two side wings, one a sharp crescent, the other a point), the pike with the flat iron point, and the spontoon (a half-pike carried by junior officers) were individual weapons. Along with swords, this arsenal provided solid protection.

a) You are an artist. Draw the weapons mentioned above. Give their names and write a paragraph about the usage of each one.

b) Naturally, I have heard about the weapons used in your century. I find them very strange, not to say terrifying. Imagine you are the editor-in-chief of an important weekly newspaper. Choose a head of production, a founder-president, two journalists and two graphic artists. Together, produce an important article for your paper entitled "Weapons of Destruction — Are They a Deterrent?" Use interesting headings, pictures, statistics and slogans. I shall be your first reader.

c) There were 10 armourers in the colony in my time. They made, repaired and sold arms. Write a text about the necessity and worth of their trade, its difficulties, and the choice they made to practise this profession.

Arbor Affinitatis

The Family

You remember that there were 12 children in our family. That wasn't at all out of the ordinary. In fact many families had 20 children and more. Women were encouraged to have as many children as possible for the most rapid growth of our population. It was from this standpoint that the arrival of the filles du Roi — daughters of the King — had been greatly welcomed. Almost 1,000 of them had arrived in New France during Intendant Talon's time. My mother had married at 12 years of age, quite an acceptable age to marry at that time. However, I did not imitate my mother on this point, because after my father's death I had to see to the business affairs of the seigneury. I was 28 when I married. That age was considered quite old for getting married.

a) The family has evolved so much since the seventeenth century that I'm sure I would hardly recognize it in your time. Let's suppose you are an author who has been asked to write an article for the magazine *The Changing World*. Your aim is to show your readers the differences and the similarities between the families of my time and yours. Think about people you know and about their family life.

b) Make your own family tree. To help yourself, put together some written and oral information. Ask questions of your family members, find old documents, photographs and newspaper clippings. Rummage through the old trunks up in the attic or down in the basement. (Ask permission first.)

c) Prepare a skit about a family in another country. Your group must present the scene with respect and with attention to detail, taking into account the local customs and the habits of the family you are portraying.

Madeleine de Verchères   From the statue by Hébert

Heroines and Heroes

Since ancient times, civilizations have needed heroines and heroes. We often need to respect, admire, flatter and even idolize people who seem "larger than life." It is thus that Greek mythology and Roman history are full of accounts of wars and adventures which feature heroines and heroes who are more or less invincible. Sometimes these stories relate exploits of people who are superhuman — or almost godlike: have you ever heard of Hercules and his efforts, for example?

a) You have heroes and heroines in your century. I know that well, my friend. Has the type of person whom we call a hero or a heroine changed much — or is it the result, the product that is different, while the process stays the same? That's a difficult question. Think about it, however, and find six people of your time who are considered heroes or heroines. Use the following headings to classify them: name, age, kind of achievement, motivation, result, consequence of the achievement. Try to find common elements in the last three columns. *Bon courage*, and good luck! It's not a Herculean task I'm setting you here.

b) My story remained hidden in the archives in Paris, France, for almost 200 years. I don't like to think about it, but it's a fact. You have decided to write the life story of your hero or heroine so that the same fate won't happen to him or her. Find out about his or her life, and ask yourself the following questions: why did the person do the things he or she did? How did he or she prepare for the task? Is he or she like you? If yes, in what way? If no, would you like to model your behaviour on his or hers?

Garakontié meets Governor Frontenac

Garakontié
1654 - 1677

Garakontié was a hero to many of his Onondaga followers. Although he was not born a chief, he became well-known and respected for his wisdom, pragmatism and integrity. He was a lover of peace and an upholder of his Iroquois traditions. Realizing that the French colony was expanding in territory and power, and that his people were dying from war and diseases brought by the colonists, he decided to negotiate. He befriended Simon Le Moyne, a Jesuit priest and another lover of peace. Prisoners were returned in good faith. Garakontié did not become a Christian, however, but did protect Simon Le Moyne from harm.

In 1661, Garakontié helped negotiate a truce between the western Iroquois and the French. Once more, prisoners were returned. Iroquois lands and rights had to be respected, he maintained; they would not be sacrificed. In 1673, he and other Iroquois leaders met with Governor Frontenac who marvelled at the eloquence and shrewdness of the Native diplomats. Real peace was still 23 years away however, and Garakontié did not live to see it.

a) It is 1673. In a group, assume the roles of Garakontié, Governor Frontenac, two accompanying followers of each, and perhaps an interpreter. Together, write a dialogue such as would be appropriate to their meeting. Remember that both the content and style are important. Rehearse it well and present it to the class.

b) Do you know of other peacemakers from your century or past centuries? Choose two, a man and a woman, and draw a pen portrait of them. Don't forget to state the outcome of their endeavours.

c) Traditions are important to many races and groups of people. With a friend, create a cartoon — one of you being the scriptwriter, the other the visual artist — that depicts respect for and pride in a certain tradition. (I hear you have such a thing in your century as a musical play in which there is a song called "Tradition." Try to find out about the song. The play is about a violinist who sits on top of a house, I believe.)

A letter written in October, 1699, by Marie-Magdeleine Jarret de Verchères.

Homage

When you speak of homage, you immediately think of respect, esteem and veneration. In my case homage is what the priests paid to my memory at my funeral. In the case of the fealty and homage the seigneur paid to the king's representative, or the habitant paid to the seigneur, we distinguished between *l'hommage simple* and *l'hommage lige*. This last term tied the habitant more closely to the seigneur, by means of a very binding contract.

a) Have you ever paid homage to someone? How did you go about it? What was the reason? What was the result of this gesture? Write a text about this subject and present it orally to your group. Speak sincerely, and I'm sure your friends will appreciate what you tell them.

b) And now, my friend, design a series of six postage stamps which represent the lives of six very remarkable people to whom we could pay homage. The people can be from different times and of different nationalities; their achievements also will vary. Send your finished product to Canada Post, Ottawa. (I believe that is what you call the service.)

c) I remember the words my father spoke so often: "Noblemen are born only to spill their blood in the service of God and king." Do you think these words justify the homage paid to me at my funeral? Write a little text on that subject.

Au revoir, my dear friend.

Marie-Magdelaine Jarret de Verchères

Angélique Leblanc

En Pennsylvanie,
le 6 avril 1756

My dear Reader,

My name is Angélique Leblanc. I am sure that my story is going to affect you, so I would like us to work together to find out why such a dreadful event occurred in my lifetime. How can we rid ourselves of the ignorance, fear and greed which lead to such disasters? How can we escape the iron fist of power? Stay close by me, while I recount the sad story of Acadia. Face up to the English soldiers with me. Learn the truth. Feel the anger and despair that I feel as the innocent victim. Then you will also recognize the mixed feelings of frustration and disbelief that I still have, along with the resignation to surmount them.

Angélique Leblanc

My dear reader, I am going to tell you a story that is true and poignant, and that dates from 1755. Please forgive me and be patient with me if my sorrow becomes too great and I find it hard to continue. I am only human, after all, and the events of that autumn still haunt me.

I am an Acadian. Do you know what that means? It means that I am French and Catholic, and that I was born in the east of the country, probably into a farming family. Acadian means that, and yet it means more. I come from a people who are very proud of their heritage, proud of their ancestors who came from the province of Poitou south of the River Loire in France. We Acadians have been able to keep our language and customs partly because we have lived as an isolated group. It is not just by chance that we became fiercely independent, patient when faced with adversity and courageous in misfortune. These traits are the result of events born out of ignorance, fear and greed.

It was a beautiful September evening. The fields covered with kelp — that wonderful seaweed we used to help the sandy soil — seemed almost golden in the late sun. Our little thatched houses seemed asleep after their busy day. Here was I, just 16 and quite pretty I think, with brown hair. They said I was as bright as the flax flowers, and as lively as the *gaspéreaux* (a kind of herring) in the Minas Basin. I was in love. I didn't know whether to choose Vincent or Antoine. What a choice! I weighed the two in my heart: one was big and strong with clear, blue eyes; the other was smaller with a smiling face and a slim body. Maybe I would choose Antoine. I imagined our life together: I would be taking care of the house, he would be coming home from the fields or the sea in the evening. He would kiss me gently on the cheek and take me by the hand to the cradle where our baby son would smile up at us with his father's engaging smile. So I would dream on, sitting on the doorstep of our home looking out onto the bay, all the while twisting and stretching the hemp on the distaff, as if in a trance.

Suddenly the alarm rings out! Nine o'clock! I didn't realize that was the time. I don't like that bell ringing in the evening. Its message is short and troubling to me. Ah, here come my parents returning from the dike. They look harassed. What's the matter with them?

"Good evening Mother, Father. You seem worried, both of you."

"Yes indeed, Angélique, I'm all out of breath. We have just got the news. Tomorrow morning, all the men from Grand Pré have to assemble in the church. It's by order of the English colonel. I just said to your father that I have never liked those English ships in the basin. They have always bothered me. Look at them down there so powerful and threatening. What's going to happen?"

"Don't worry, Mother. What can they do to us? This is our country, our native land. We're all friends here. What do you think, Father?"

But my father replied only with a solemn shake of the head. He went slowly into the house. A sadness had entered him.

Next morning the whole family was up early. The young ones, their faces tanned by the long summer, their eyes full of fun and mischief, ran about seeing to their chores: my younger sister went off to pick vegetables, my brother got ready to fish for shad. My father, thoughtful and silent, was still seated at the big rough-hewn table. He was watching my mother knead the bread for supper. She was pregnant for the seventh time. She moved slowly these days, and last night's events had clearly tired her out. She had dark circles under her eyes and her skin was sallow. My father noticed these things. She glanced towards him, went to speak, but determined to remain silent, knowing that any question at this time would be useless.

What's that noise? Did you hear that? Listen! They're drums, soldiers' drums. And there goes that bell again! My father gets up quickly, glances almost secretly at my mother, and leaves. He goes out into the most beautiful, calm and sun-filled morning, a morning to live a thousand mornings.

More drums! Come, come with me, my friend. You will be part of my story. Let's follow my father along the path, past Antoine's house, and on to the little slope that leads down to the church. Here we are. What a lot of people! Whole families are here! The church doors are wide open. Look, the men are entering the church one by one, pushed by the English soldiers. My father's going in too. "Father! Father!" He doesn't hear me. Old Monsieur Comeaux is last to go in, his iron-tipped stick tapping on the flagstones. The soldiers' uniforms, shining brilliantly in the morning sunshine, also disappear into the gloom of the church. The doors are shut! Look around us. No one is moving, no one is speaking. Even the children are absolutely still. "Maman...maman!" a little one cries out. He is afraid. What's happening inside?

The English colonel is issuing this proclamation:

Men of Grand Pré, listen well to this proclamation! You have rejected the new oath of allegiance to your sovereign. Here therefore are his orders: as from today, all of your lands, your houses and your herds are confiscated in the name of the Crown. As for you and your families, you will be transported far from this place. We hope that the future holds peace for you. You are now prisoners!

I hear the men shouting inside the church. What is it? Here comes the commanding officer, a parchment in his hands. He is going to read from it. You please listen for me, my friend; I can't hear what he has to say, or I don't want to. He is talking about our leaving Grand Pré, our leaving this country in three days' time, our belongings piled on the shore, aboard English ships! No! No! No! We can't! We can't! Run home, find Mother!

"Mother, Mother! Father is in the church with Antoine and the others. We have to leave our home in three days. We have to leave our country aboard English ships!"

"Angélique, I knew that something bad was going on. I do not think we have a choice. Let's get ready. Call the children."

My mother had already shed her tears of grief and anger. Now it was my turn. I ran outside, shouting out the names of the children, "Étienne! Marie!" My voice was hoarse, my sobs seemed to wring out my throat. My Antoine is down there. I love him, I love him!

During the next three days, my mother and I and our little Leblanc brood tried to gather together our possessions. We piled some furniture onto an old cart. How long would we be

207

away? Where were we going? We had no answers to those questions. On the last day, we said goodbye to our home, and we made our way toward the shore, the little ones clutching their precious toys, the older ones carrying provisions for the journey. My mother walked with difficulty, but she did not complain. It was a solemn procession which wound its way slowly toward the water. We had just reached the shore when the heavy church doors opened wide, and the men — our men — came into view, saddened and downtrodden. Resignation and despair showed on their faces.

There's Father! "Father! Father! We're over here. Come!" He kissed us, and we saw the tears in his eyes. My mother took him in her arms, and practical as always, asked if he was hungry. Our breakfast table was a box made of maple, our kitchen floor a pebbly shore. The autumn morning was misty as we sat down as a family to partake of one of the last meals we were to have in our beloved Acadia.

All that day and the next, boats filled with people and provisions plied between the shore and the ships. Antoine went off in one, Vincent in another. Our family was luckier than most and managed to stay together. From the ship we could see a reddish glow which filled the sky above Grand Pré. As the smoke and flames of our burning homes became more intense, the English ships with their human cargo weighed anchor, and sailed toward the open water. Our destination was Pennsylvania. We never came back.

The Mi'kmaq Nation

The Mi'kmaq nation occupied the territory known to you in your century as Nova Scotia, Prince Edward Island and eastern New Brunswick. In Newfoundland lived the Beothuk nation. All of those Native peoples had had their own beliefs, laws, and special way of life for centuries before the arrival of us, the Europeans.

They used what their environment had to offer, regarding the air, earth and water as common gifts to be appreciated then left for the next generation. The Mi'kmaqs fished for eel, trout, salmon, halibut, cod and mackerel. Oysters, lobsters, clams, seals and walrus completed their harvest from the sea. Their canoes were made of birchbark, hand-crafted with care and skill. They hunted beaver, moose, bear and caribou using the traps, harpoons and bows and arrows they had fashioned.

A boy would be considered a man when he had hunted down his first animal, showing that he could now support a family. A girl was considered a woman when she could accomplish various tasks, for example cooking, weaving carpets and baskets, scraping, tanning and smoking hides. Their homes were wigwams which were covered with woven rattan or perhaps grass. The rattan shrank in dry weather thus allowing for good air circulation. It expanded in the dampness so preventing rain from entering. During the winter, the wigwams were covered with birchbark. They were round, oval or triangular, and inside, each person had his or her own place so that a type of privacy could be maintained.

As for music, bone flutes, bark drums and fish-skinned rattles were played for dancing. Singing and storytelling were always popular as entertainment and as a learning experience for the young people. Elders were respected and listened to, diseases were treated with natural remedies, burial rites were accorded to all. It was into this picture that the Europeans sailed, gradually changing the way of life of the Mi'kmaqs forever.

a)   Find more information in your library on the Mi'kmaq nation. In a group, discuss what you have read, and state the positive and negative results of the white man's arrival on Mi'kmaq soil, from your point of view.

b)   You are a Mi'kmaq. You and your family are seated around the central fire inside your wigwam home. Your grandfather or grandmother starts to tell a story. Everyone listens intently. Write this story, making it suitable for the time and place. Rehearse it, and read it to your group.

c)   Draw a series of six postage stamps which depict the way of life of the Mi'kmaqs. Try to be as accurate and as artistic as possible. Send your finished product to Canada Post with a covering letter. (I believe that is what the service is called.) Good luck! *Bonne chance!*

A Mi'kmaq prayer book

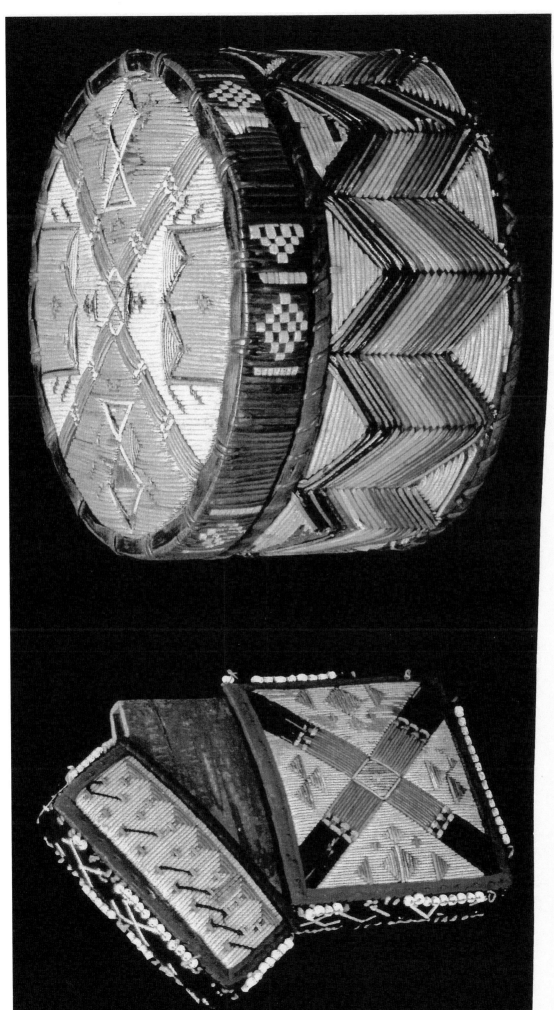

A Mi'kmaq calling card case and box

Matthieu Da Costa, who died in 1607, was a Black interpreter for Samuel de Champlain.

Matthieu Da Costa

15?- 1607

In 1606, two years after the first French landing in the area, Matthieu Da Costa sailed to Port-Royal with Jean de Poutrincourt, Marc Lescarbot who was a lawyer, poet and scholar, and Louis Hébert, the apothecary and farmer. Matthieu Da Costa was different from the other hand-picked settlers in two regards — he already had a fine knowledge of the language of the Mi'kmaq people, and he was a Black man.

We do not know the facts of his earlier life. Perhaps he had been brought over to this continent as a slave on a Portuguese sailing ship. He must then have lived with the Mi'kmaqs or traded with them to learn their language. Perhaps he bought his freedom or escaped, but one thing is certain — he was in Paris, France, when Jean de Poutrincourt decided to sail. After arriving in Port-Royal, Matthieu Da Costa became Samuel de Champlain's own interpreter, and explored the eastern coast with him. He was a link in the relationship between the French and the Mi'kmaqs. Alas, barely a year later he died of scurvy as did so many others. He was the first African-American (to use the term from your century) to set foot on our soil.

d) You are a television journalist who is interviewing Matthieu Da Costa, Samuel de Champlain and a representative of the Mi'kmaq nation. Prepare your questions well and make sure they are clear and pertinent. Have your group present the program to the class. I shall listen with interest.

e) I believe it is advantageous to be able to speak languages other than one's maternal tongue. Write a paragraph affirming or refuting this point of view, giving examples to support your words.

f) In your library you will find information on many other African-Americans who have contributed in some way to the life and well-being of their communities large and small. Choose one woman and one man, and write an article based on their lives under the heading: "Making a Difference." It is for a well-known newspaper, so choose your vocabulary carefully.

"The 1604 expedition to Canada was led by Pierre de Monts, who had been given the trade monopoly for New France. One of the main aims of the venture was the establishment of a rich trade for France in Acadian furs."

Acadia in the Seventeenth Century

French colonists under Pierre de Gua, Sieur de Monts and Samuel de Champlain began to settle in the area to be known as Acadia as early as 1604. The first site chosen by about 80 of them was a small island at the mouth of the Sainte-Croix River: alas, 35 of them perished that winter. The following year, some of them crossed French Bay — the Baie Française to us, the Bay of Fundy to you — to settle on the south shore in the Port-Royal Basin. In 1607, Sieur de Monts returned to France with all of his companions, and three years later, another group of French colonists came to Port-Royal. However, England had had its eyes on this territory for some time: in 1613, Samuel Argall took possession of Acadia, renamed Nova Scotia a few years later. France regained the land in 1632, and named Isaac de Razilly as lieutenant general and governor of the new colony. On his death, MM. Latour and d'Aulnay argued over his succession. At the same time, French-English rivalry was heating up. Before the end of the century, Acadia had changed hands four more times.

g)   Research one of the historical characters mentioned above. Write an account of his ambitions and exploits during this troubled period.

h)   Imagine you are one of the first colonists to land on Sainte-Croix Island. Conditions are dreadful, the winter of 1604-1605 is particularly harsh, scurvy is rampant. As a group, write a skit based on this scenario using any other information you can find in the library.

i)   Find an old map of Acadia. Study it carefully with a friend and compare it to a modern map as to the names of the bays, islands, rivers and various localities. Now the whole group can try to recreate a map of this area in the seventeenth century. Don't forget the compass points, the scale and the legend.

You can probably come to the conclusion, my friend, that the French-English struggle had terrible consequences, and that it was indeed ominous for the future of the colony and its inhabitants. Let's reconstruct the painful events that followed. Come with me to see Acadia, to see my country.

Ré - veille ré - veille c'est

les sol - dats qui viennent, Brûl -

er - la ré - colte Ré -

veille ré - veille,

hommes - a - cad - iens Pour

sauv - er le vill - age. Mon

grand grand grand grand - père ...

Réveille

"Réveille" is a song which depicts the indomitable Acadian spirit maintained in spite of the terrible events which took place between the years 1755 and 1762. It does not come from my time, in fact it comes from yours. Try to find a copy. I have heard speak of its beauty, simplicity and strength. It is based on a thorough knowledge of the situation, and a real sensitivity to the suffering of the people in it. Zachary Richard from Louisiana wrote the words. The writing of this song reflects a new and lively interest in all areas of Acadian culture, in its survival and its growth. A real *réveil*, a real "awakening" is taking place, not only among Acadians but in the general populace. Edith Butler has made a recording of the song.

a) Together with your friends, stage a little play in which the theme depicts the events outlined in the song or in my story. Choose a producer, a director, actors, makeup artists and costume designers — and don't forget to build simple sets and find props to make your scenes more realistic. First discuss the text, then step boldly onto the stage, have several rehearsals, and present the result of your efforts to the class.

b) And now, my friend, it's your turn to write a musical composition. Write a simple little melody. Sing it over, and give it words which are meaningful to you, or even play it on your favourite instrument (flute, piano, harmonica, guitar, violin...). Tape your work and give it to the person of your choice. I can't wait to hear it.

c) Find other musical compositions — songs or instrumental pieces — which depict sad or happy events. Categorize them using the following headings: event, country, date, main characters, composer, reason for the work, listeners' feelings.

"TREE OF AFFINITIES was used in medieval times to determine the relation that a husband and a wife each bears to the kin of the other. The illustration, a woodcut made in 1473 by Johannes Andrei, is reproduced with the permission of the Pierpont Morgan Library."

The Name of Acadia

The word *Acadie* means "Acadia," and can be found in many songs, tales, legends and stories dating from my time. In fact it is the name given to the first French colony on this continent. We think it goes back to Verrazano, the Italian navigator who was in the service of France. Noticing the lovely eastern coastline on a voyage which brought him as far as this continent, he named it *Arcadie* because of the "beauty of its trees." The word *Arcadie* comes from ancient Greece, where it referred to a plain on the Peloponnesus known for its beautiful greenery. Somewhere between then and now *Arcadie* lost its *r*, and the map-makers of the sixteenth century called the whole area bordering on the ocean *Acadie*.

a) I have heard it said that in your century there are provinces and territories the names of which are characteristic of their areas, their inhabitants, or their former political systems. Name the provinces and territories of your country and write the origins of their names alongside. Good research at the library will yield some surprising results.

b) Create an imaginary country (in my time we also said Utopia: an imaginary land with an ideal government where the people lived happily). Draw a map of it and describe it in detail: situation, relief, waterways, climate, vegetation, natural resources and population. Give it a name. Would you like to live there? Justify your answer.

c) In 1671, Acadia had already many families. Among them were the names of Blanchard, Boudrot, Bourgeois, Brot, Comeaux, Cormier, Daigre, Doucet, Landry, Leblanc, Mélanson, Poirier, Richard, Robichaud, and Thibaudeau. Family names were very important to the colonists because they had brought very little else from France. They were very proud of their heritage. Now it's *your* turn to find out about your family as you construct your own family tree. Learn about your family from asking questions of your parents, grand-parents, aunts, uncles and cousins. Look carefully at any documents which have been kept by your family: old letters and photographs, newspaper clippings, diplomas, and even — if you're lucky — diaries.

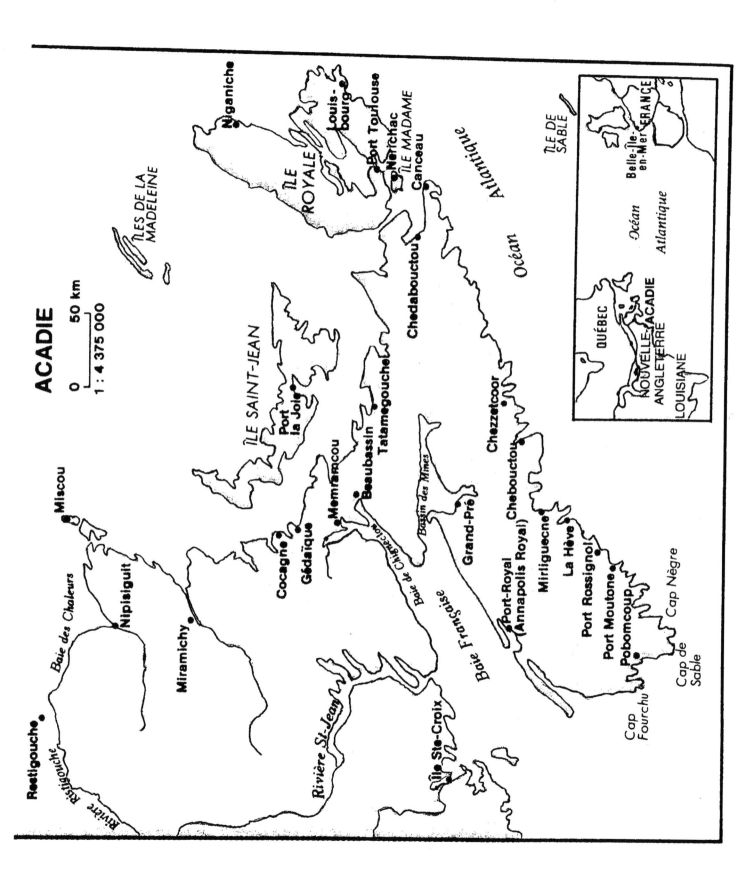

ACADIE

0   50 km

1 : 4 375 000

Restigouche

Rivière Restigouche

Baie des Chaleurs

Nipisiguit

Miscou

Miramichy

ÎLES DE LA MADELEINE

Niganiche

ÎLE ROYALE

Louis-bourg

Port Toulouse

Nérichac
ÎLE MADAME
Canceau

Océan   Atlantique

ÎLE DE SABLE

ÎLE SAINT-JEAN

Port la Joie

Cocagne

Gédaïque

Memramcou

Beaubassin

Tatamagouche

Baie de Chignictou

Bassin des Mines

Chedabouctou

Chezzetcoor

Chebouctou

Grand-Pré

Baie Française

Rivière St-Jean

Île Ste-Croix

Port-Royal
(Annapolis Royal)

Mirliguecne

La Hève

Port Rossignol

Port Moutone

Pobomcoup

Cap de Sable

Cap Nègre

Cap Fourchu

QUÉBEC

NOUVELLE-
ANGLETERRE

ACADIE

FRANCE

Belle-île-en-Mer

Océan   Atlantique

LOUISIANE

The Region of Acadia

The region of Acadia passed into English hands in 1713. The document that marks this event is the Treaty of Utrecht, which stated that the word *Acadia* meant "Acadia in its old sense," as to its boundaries. However, the French and English could never agree on these boundaries. The French thought the region was only the peninsula of Nova Scotia; the English understood it to extend to the west (New Brunswick in your time), to the northwest (the Gaspé Peninsula) and even to the southwest (the State of Maine, I believe). In spite of this dispute, France kept two islands, Île Saint-Jean (later to be Prince Edward Island) and Île Royale (Cape Breton Island). Île Saint-Jean became an important fishing centre, while Île Royale assumed a role of defence.

a)   With one of your friends, write a dialogue between two administrators, one French, the other English. Have them discuss quite assertively but politely the Acadian territorial boundaries. Write out the contents of the dialogue, have several rehearsals and present the little scene to the class.

b)   Draw two maps of the area. They must indicate the different Acadian territorial boundaries as seen by the French and the English. Include everything I noted above, and add the following place names: Port-Royal, Grand Pré, Les Mines and Beaubassin (the last three founded between the years 1670 and 1680).

Old Fort, near Annapolis Royal

French and Catholic

The French recognized British authority over us, the Acadians of Port-Royal, Grand Pré, Les Mines and Beaubassin. It was the French who wanted us to go and settle in the fortress town of Louisbourg, which still belonged to them. We refused to heed them on this point. How could we abandon our fertile lands and our homes? We had come here in 1630, 1640 and 1650, and we regarded this land as our own, whatever power we were under. We looked after our own daily needs by growing crops, rearing animals, hunting, fishing, and trafficking in furs.

However, our English masters soon realized that we held fast to our French heritage and our faith. They distrusted both. Where would our sympathies lie if a war broke out between New France and the British colony? The British could not be sure of our support. Hadn't the Native peoples themselves made agreements with us, and weren't they allies of the French? The English thought of us in this way, and I can understand that, at least up to a certain point: we were almost 15,000 Acadians beside a handful of English colonists.

a) You are an Englishman of high rank living at Port-Royal — now called Annapolis Royal. Your job is to write a report to the English government across the ocean. Describe the situation as you see it, express your opinion as clearly as possible, and offer some suggestions for the future of the region. (You have the right to propose different solutions from those chosen by the administration of the time.)

b) Draw up a list of the advantages and disadvantages for the Acadians of being administered by the French or the English. Were there really great differences between the two regimes? Think carefully about this important question. Your reply will interest me greatly.

c) Think of some situations from your century which are similar to ours of the eighteenth century. Unfortunately you will find examples from all over the world. What are the origins of those numerous conflicts? Are they religious, linguistic, ethnic or political? Discuss this in a group, and try to predict the outcome of those conflicts not already resolved.

The North West View of Fort Lawrence in Chignectou 1755

1 Block houses.
2 Command. quarters.
3 Officers' quarters.
4 Soldiers' barracks.
5 Commissary quarters.
6 Line of tall Pallisades.
7 Mr. Martins.
8 The Fives Court.
9 Command.ts Summer h.
10 Dittos Stable.
11 Brewh.+Mr. Hustons
12 formerly Mr. Glazier.

Fort Lawrence, 1755

The British Point of View

In order to resolve problems of language and religion — and also to appease our mistrust of the English — the English themselves proposed the concept of an elected assembly to be controlled by us. In reality, we soon realized that those elected were in the pay of our masters. As for the taxes that the English demanded to cover the administrative costs of the colony, we succeeded in ignoring them in one way or another. And if we were on plots of land reserved for the English colonists, it was *us* who had constructed the dikes to make that land more fertile.

Similarly, the English laws forbade in principle the practice of our religion, Roman Catholicism, but did allow its exercise in Acadia. However, in spite of all attempts at appeasement, British politics failed us badly. The English wanted to be sure of our loyalty, and so in 1713 they demanded an oath of allegiance from us. We absolutely refused, wanting to remain true to our ideal of neutrality, to our faith and our past. In 1730, Governor Philipps gave his word on one of our claims: we could remain neutral (like Switzerland in your century).

a) You are presenting a television newscast (1 hear you have such an invention in your time). Choose two friends, and working together, create a program about the events of 1730 in which Governor Philipps and an Acadian delegate are interviewed by a journalist. The journalist asks pertinent questions on the information given above. The replies must be as detailed and as interesting as possible as your audience could be very large. Present the program to the class.

b) Have you ever sworn an oath to a person, an organization or an institution? If you have, write a page in your diary describing the circumstances, and the feelings you had at that time. If you have not, ask someone who has become a citizen of your country to tell you his or her story, and report it in your journal.

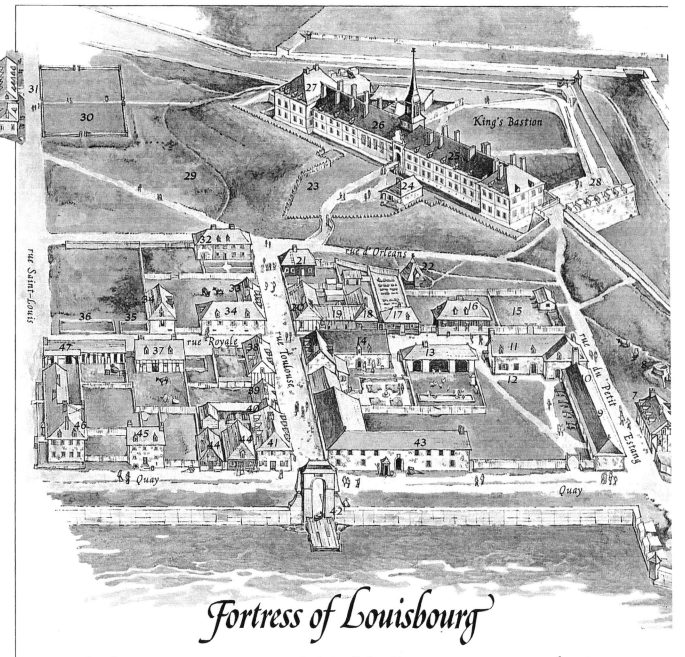

Fortress of Louisbourg

1. Dauphin Gate
2. Epéron Battery
3. Dauphin Demi-bastion
4. Powder Magazine
5. Barracks
6. Postern Tunnel
7. Lartigue House
8. Lime Kiln
9. Artillery Storehouse
10. Artillery Forge
11. Armoury and Armourer's Forge
12. King's Bakery
13. Laundry and Stables
14. Engineer's Residence
15. Wood Yard
16. Duhaget House (t) (r)
17. De la Perelle House (t)

18. De la Perelle Storehouse
19. Rodrigue Storehouse
20. Rodrigue House
21. De Gannes House
22. Icehouse
23. Place d'armes
24. Guardhouse
25. Soldiers' Barracks (&)
26. Chapel
27. Governor's Apartments
28. Ramparts
29. Place Royale
30. King's Garden
31. Museum
32. De la Plagne House (t) (&)
33. De la Vallière House
34. De la Vallière Storehouses

35. Loppinot House Ruins
36. Fizel House Ruins
37. Dugas-de la Tour House
38. Carrerot House
39. Benoist House
40. L'Epée Royale (✗)
41. Hôtel de la Marine (✗)
42. Frédéric Gate
43. King's Storehouse
44. Grandchamp Houses
45. Destouches House (✗)
46. Ordonnateur's Residence (t) (r)
47. Stables

(t) Theme Lounges
(✗) Restaurant
(r) Rest Rooms (&) Accessible Rest Room

The Fortress of Louisbourg

In 1720, the French began the construction of Louisbourg, the fortress-town on Île Royale (Cape Breton Island). Its situation was a strategic one. The French wanted to protect their main approach to New France from English attacks. Unfortunately for them, however, very few Acadians took up the offer to settle there. This did not prevent the officers at the fortress from considering all French colonists compatriots faithful to the fleur-de-lys.[*]

In 1745, William Shirley, Governor of Massachusetts, launched a surprise attack on Louisbourg. The British navy joined in, and the siege of the town lasted 48 days. The French governor, Duchambon, finally surrendered after the destruction of the town and the fortress. Henceforth the British controlled the whole of the Gulf of St. Lawrence, so ships coming from France were at great risk. Accordingly, the fur trade grew smaller, while the English trading flourished. Happily, Louisbourg did not stay in enemy hands for long: the fortress was returned to the French at the end of the War of Austrian Succession. It was given back to France in exchange for the colony of Madras in India, which was of more interest to Great Britain.

a) Find out more about Louisbourg, then do a mini-project on it as it was in my time, with maps, drawings and diagrams of all kinds.

b) You are a French soldier stationed at Louisbourg in 1745. Write a letter to your parents in France describing the surprise attack and the subsequent siege. Do extra research to enable you to depict these events clearly and accurately. Your feelings as a soldier must be conveyed also. Perhaps you could suggest some strategy for the future.

c) Find out information about four other famous sieges that have taken place anywhere in the world at any time. Categorize them using the following headings: country, date, place under siege, people involved, reasons for the siege, length of the siege, and outcome.

---

[*] You can find the fleur-de-lys in pictures of the royal arms of France in my day, and before my time. It is the flag of the province of Quebec in your century.

A modern re-enactment at a restored Louisbourg

A modern re-enactment at a restored Louisbourg

Sunlit kitchen on a Sunday afternoon entices two servants of the de Gannes House to relax after a week

The Acadian Woman's Role

Life was rather hard for us Acadian women. No matter what regime we were under — English or French — daily life brought its usual tasks, household chores and trials. Generally, we had to marry at a young age, about 16, and we had lots of children. That was the fate of us women. When you married a good-natured, fine young man who was hard-working and light of heart, then everything was for the best in the best of Acadias. On the other hand, if a worthless character, lazy and miserable, came to ask your father for your hand, and if, misfortune of misfortunes, your father accepted for you, your life at his farm would not be a rosy one, believe me.

As for me, I had chosen Antoine as my future husband as you know, and he had just decided to talk to my father when those sad events took place. I had already begun to prepare all my treasures, wool cloth and linen sheets woven with patience, skill and affection. I well knew that my days as a wife and mother would be filled with work, but I knew too that they would bring me joy and satisfaction. I would have meals to prepare, flax and hemp to weave, clothes to wash and sew and sew again, the vegetable garden to look after, provisions to lay in for the long winter months, the children to bring up and care for.... But Antoine and I would be happy surrounded by our beautiful youngsters who would grow up on our dear Acadian soil — or so we dreamed.

a) Describe the day of an Acadian woman who is married with eight children.
b) According to you, what qualities would be necessary in a husband or wife to help him or her live happily and successfully on an Acadian farm in the eighteenth century? Compare these qualities to what you might hope to find in *your* future companion. Make up two lists under the headings: then, now.
c) Create a skit based on family life in Acadia at the beginning of the eighteenth century. Working in a group, choose a producer, a director and actors. Try to make the atmosphere as real and alive as possible. Don't hesitate to use objects or tools of the period for props (or at least those that you have made). Enjoy your production!

Construction of the Acadian dike

Old Marshes, New Dikes

We Acadians were a realistic people; consider the numerous dikes we built when we realized their practical value. Settled as we were along the rivers which flowed into the Bay of Fundy — the Baie Française, in our time — we were faced with very high tides. When the water ebbed, it left large areas of marshland behind it. Now, we had noticed that once these lands had dried and were salt-free, they were excellent for growing crops. So, our menfolk constructed dikes to contain the sea so well that from then on we had abundant, fertile lands. (That is one of the reasons the British wanted to take our lands and give them to the English and Scottish colonists, that's for sure.)

We had two methods of constructing the dikes, one where trunks of trees were placed deep into the soil, and blocks of wood were piled horizontally with a type of thick clay acting as a cement; the other where clayey turf was cut into large squares and piled up to a height of five feet or so above the marshes. We had made a discharge channel in the middle of each marsh that allowed the water to flow away without necessarily letting the sea come in. It was hard work which took several days, but the men took to their task with enthusiasm, helping each other without complaining. The following year's harvest paid us back for our efforts. And in time, the dikes became covered in grass and served as paths for us to walk on.

a) Find information on dikes of other countries, and make a series of drawings of four of them. The drawings should be well labelled. Above each dike, indicate its location, and the reason why it was constructed.

b) What is a dam? Find some illustrations — photographs, drawings or postcards — whereby you can make a collage to show some of the best dams of your time. Write the names of the dams shown and find information on their size, situation, and construction.

233

Francis Swaine (1735-1782)

A BRITISH MAN OF WAR IN CALM WATERS OFF THE COAST

Oil on canvas
30 by 45cm.; 11 ¾ by 17 ¾ in.

The Threatening Presence

An odd threat seemed to hang over us when we looked out at the English ships in our basin. As you know, Halifax was founded in 1749 by the English. One of the clear advantages of Halifax was its situation: the English now had an excellent seaport. The seat of government was no longer in Annapolis Royal (the former Port-Royal), but far away from the Acadian communities which depended on its jurisdiction.

Wanting to make the whole peninsula as English as possible, the British government used every effort to attract "good" colonists, that means colonists who would support them in their plans. Most of the new arrivals were to come from New England and from German territories under British rule, like Hanover and Brunswick. Between the years 1750 and 1760, more than 7,000 of these colonists settled in the former Acadia. As early as 1750, the French replied to this British initiative by building Fort Beauséjour, to be answered by the construction of Fort Lawrence by the British barely two and a half miles to the east.* We, the Acadian people, were in a very difficult situation: the English administration wanted our lands for its colonists; we didn't speak the same language; we practised a religion it abhorred. We were called stubborn!

a)   Let's create a court trial. Working in a group, choose a judge, a representative of the Crown (to act against the accused), a lawyer (to defend him), a jury of several members, and of course the accused person. The British Crown has put an Acadian on trial because he or she has refused to give up his or her land to a colonist recently arrived from Massachusetts. The jury must give its verdict at the close of the trial, after hearing the accused, the representative of the Crown, and the defence counsel. Present the whole scene to the class.

b)   You are a writer. Compose an Acadian legend that could have been passed from generation to generation, and that has as its theme the peaceful time before the arrival of the British. Write the legend, then read it to the class with a background of Acadian music. (You will find tapes of Edith Butler, Angèle Arsenault, Donat Lacroix or the group Beausoleil Broussard in your local library or at your music store: "La Chanson de la cuiller" is a good example of a lovely song about the hardships of my people.)

---

* As you know, one of our miles is the same as 1.6 km in your day.

" A 1578 tally of vessels off the coast of the New Found Land reads "over 100 saile of Spaniards . . . 20 or 30 from Biskaie . . . of Portugals above 50 . . . of the French nation and the Britons about 150." The fish they were catching was mostly cod, prepared in two ways: the "green-cod" method of cleaning, salting and pressing the fish into barrels; and the English "dry-cod" method above. The catch here is cleaned on covered "stages," then spread on "flakes" to dry.

Fishing

Thanks to our geographical situation, we received a heaven-sent gift — fish. From the beginning of our settling in Acadia, our menfolk had used dams made from stakes driven into the river bed. These stretched across the river, preventing the fish that had come up with the tide from escaping once the tide ebbed. We salted these fish and dried them in the sun on the roofs of our homes. This method was also used by the coastal fishermen who cut their fish into triangular shapes and spread them out on frames to dry. This technique for preserving fish was called *la pêche sèche*; as for *la pêche fraîche*, it meant that the fish were salted and piled into casks on board the fishing boats. These boats came from the Old World to fish for cod near our shores. The fishermen from New England also had access to these fertile waters. Imagine what our men could have done, being so close to this marine harvest! But they were happy with their modest catch: shad, sardine, perch, plaice, *gaspéreau* (a kind of herring). After all, that was all they needed for themselves and their families. They also fished for cod at Port-Royal, but not in the Minas Basin.

a) For centuries the Grand Banks have seen fishermen arrive from across the ocean. Form a group of your friends, and do a study of the Grand Banks in my century or before. Each member of the group will have a designated task, for example finding the countries of origin, the types of vessels used, the facts about life on-board ship, and the methods of fishing and preserving. Each person's contribution to the study will be discussed and integrated into the whole. Maps, drawings, diagrams and short texts will make this project interesting when you present it to the class.

b) Do some research on the Native peoples' fishing methods. Find out how these methods were so suited to the environment. Try to make a few sketches to illustrate these different methods, and write short explanations alongside.

PRODUCT OF FRANCE
White Wine

Vouvray

a light, delicate flavour and bouquet

Produce and Livestock

We were really very lucky; the harvests from our fields rivalled the produce from the sea in their bounty. The marshland that we had surrounded by dikes proved wonderful for crops. We grew enough wheat, corn, rye, oats and peas for our own needs and for export. We had planted lots of fruit trees, especially apple trees (oh, the marvellous cider we would make from our apples), pear and cherry trees. And we had many different kinds of vegetables: cabbages, parsnips, onions, carrots, turnips, beetroots, chives, lettuces and all sorts of herbs to flavour the dishes.

As for our livestock, everyone knew that our oxen, sheep, lambs and fowl were of the best quality — and very cheap. As the area was also good for game, our menfolk often brought home hares and partridges which added greatly to the normal fare. In fact, we were able to see to our own needs, thanks to a very generous Mother Nature.

a) Compare Acadia, my native land, to the Maritime provinces, from the point of view of agriculture and livestock. Start by making a list of the similarities and differences, then write an account based on the information you have.

b) Create three recipes that could have been used in my home in Grand Pré. You can use only what would have been available at that time. The meals are for a family of ten, and they must be nourishing and appetizing. Write each recipe on a card, and when the whole group or class has finished, classify the recipes according to their content and size (appetizer, main course, salad, dessert). Send the best or the most interesting ones to a publisher, newspaper, food magazine or restaurant specializing in our food. *Bon appétit!*

c) The Acadians quenched their thirst with *eau d'épinette*: to make this deliciously refreshing drink, we boiled young branches from the spruce tree in water and added some molasses to the juice. After that, we poured the liquid into a cask and added yeast from wheat, then we left everything to ferment and froth. We closed up the cask and didn't touch it for four days; then we could drink our fill (only when we had leisure time, and that didn't happen much). Can you find six drinks from other countries which are made from produce grown in those countries? Draw a label for the bottle of each one.

CHARLES CORNWALLIS
British general
Dec. 31, 1738 - Oct. 5, 1805

The Oath of Allegiance
1749

It was our economic independence — we could see to our own needs — that made us refuse the oath of allegiance to the British king once more. This oath clearly implied that we would support the English in the case of war with France. Each time a new English governor came, the same old question of the oath would emerge, and we would try to get out of it by referring to our neutrality. This time it was no longer a question of neutrality. Governor Cornwallis — the same one who founded Halifax — upon receiving the refusal of the Acadian delegates, acted just like we had foreseen: he did not abide by it. He threatened to deport us, but didn't carry out the threat. Maybe he thought that such a deportation would create a difficult situation for *him*, or perhaps he didn't have strong enough forces to carry it out. Anyway, our life continued to muddle along as before.

a) Why threaten us then leave us free? Give your opinion of Governor Cornwallis' strange behaviour. Form a group of cabinet ministers representing the British Crown, and discuss the situation.

b) Would you like to be a governor of a colony? Justify your answer, whether it's positive or negative.

c) You have to leave your home. For how long? Nobody knows. For what destination? Nobody knows that either. Name five personal objects that you would try to take with you. Write down your reasons for choosing these objects.

THE FLIGHT OF THE HUGUENOTS.

The "Edict of Nantes," which had been issued by Henry IV. of France in 1598, granted to the Huguenots religious and some civil liberty. In 1685, as the culmination of his centralising policy, Louis XIV. revoked the Edict. As a result a large number of Huguenots, often the most industrious and useful citizens of France, fled to Protestant countries, Prussia, whose prosperity they founded, Holland and Great Britain. The "Revolution" made a great impression on British minds, and increased the discontent with the pro-French policy of the government.

The Oath of Allegiance
1755

In 1754, war broke out on our continent. It had been brewing for many years. Charles Lawrence was the governor of the colony at that time. We found him difficult to deal with, much harder than his predecessor. He said we were unfocused in our thinking. As a military man, he could not bear the presence of more than 15,000 Acadians on his territory. After all, he couldn't trust us and he abhorred our religion. He stated that we had refused to swear an unconditional oath to the British king for almost 40 years, that we were totally under the authority of our priests, and that we gave aid to the Native peoples and provisions to the French soldiers at forts Beauséjour and Louisbourg! He could not tolerate either our attitude or our conduct. In 1754 he sent a report to London in which he wrote:

> There is no hope that the Acadian situation will improve in as much as the oath of allegiance to the Crown has not been taken. And, furthermore, they will not take that oath without being forced to do so, especially while under the influence of those troublemaking French priests.

Profiting from the presence of English warships in the Bay of Fundy — our Baie Française — as well as from the arrival of troops from New England, Sir Charles Lawrence decided to act. He demanded an unconditional oath from us. Otherwise we would be deported! He did not give our delegates much time to discuss this ultimatum. No sooner said than done! Everything started to happen! The deportation was upon us — from the end of July, 1755. Sir Charles, with the support of the English lords, had settled once and for all, or so he thought, the "Acadian question." As for us, down through the generations and in spite of our dispersion, we have never forgotten what we called simply the *grand dérangement*. (I believe you refer to it as the "deportation.")

a)   Imagine you are Governor Charles Lawrence. You are writing your autobiography, the part which covers the years from 1755-1760. Don't forget that everyone tries to justify his or her actions before the great judge of posterity — history. Try to write the text as you think he would have written it.

b)   Find other peoples who have been taken from their homelands for various reasons. Working in a group, have each member adopt the nationality or religion of one of these groups, find information about it and offer a presentation to the class.

PROVINCE of NOVA SCOTIA,

By His EXCELLENCY,

CHARLES LAWRENCE

Captain General and Governor in Chief, in and over His Majesty's Province of Nova Scotia or Accadie in America, Vice Admiral of the same.

A PROCLAMATION.

" Coat of Arms. Charles Lawrence, a military man all his life, came to Nova Scotia as a commander of a company of British soldiers stationed in the colony. Quickly making a name for himself both as administrator and soldier, he was eventually made governor. He died suddenly in Halifax in 1760. This is his coat of arms. "

New Brunswick Museum

Cha' Lawrence.

GOD Save the KING.

The Deportation — Le grand dérangement

The British government's decision had dramatic results. The English troops seized Fort Beauséjour and imprisoned all the Acadians between there and Annapolis Royal. So, Grand Pré, my home, became one of the first places to be taken. In each village, large and small, the British troops gathered the menfolk together and forced the women and children to join them on the ships. At the same time, they took all our livestock and the produce from our harvests so that those among us who had fled could not return to supply ourselves with provisions. You see, there were many of our men and women who had taken refuge in the woods, or who were fleeing to Virginia and Louisiana — up to 700 of them made it to Québec! But when some of them returned later on, all they found were British colonists on their land, and their former homes burned to the ground. They succeeded in resettling here and there along the coast. For the majority of us, however, we had begun a new life far from our *chère Acadie*.

a) Read *Evangeline*, the famous poem to be written by Henry Wadsworth Longfellow, where he would evoke the sufferings of the Acadians who were deported. This poem would be inspired by the true story of Emmeline Labiche, a young Acadian woman of this time. Discuss the text in class.

b) Let us put forward a hypothesis: let us suppose that the *grand dérangement* had not taken place, and that we, the Acadian people, had remained on our land. What would have happened then, do you think? Write down your thoughts.

c) Because we lived in isolated groups, we had little contact with the outside world right up to the end of the last century. This fact enabled us to keep our traditions, our way of speaking, our songs and tales. We have a rich folklore, one that is still very much alive. Find out about our folklore, and as a group, make a collection of the stories and music of my people.

At the second congress, held in Miscouche, Prince Edward Island, on August 15, 1884, we Acadians would choose symbols for our people — symbols that would unite us and also distinguish us from the rest of the population. Our chosen flag would be a French tricolour with a gold star in the blue section, our anthem the "Ave Maris Stella," a religious song dedicated to the Virgin Mary, sung in Latin.

Au revoir, my friend. I shall never forget you, just as I hope you will never forget my story.

Angélique Leblanc

Bibliography

Étienne Brûlé

Butterfield, Consul Willshire, 1824-1899. *Brûlé's Discoveries and Explorations*, Cleveland, Helman Taylor, 1898

Cranston, James Herbert. *Étienne Brûlé: Immortal Scoundrel*, Toronto, Ryerson Press, 1969

Champlain, Samuel de, 1567-1635. *Voyages of Samuel de Champlain*, translated from the French by Charles Pomeroy Otis, Ph.D., with historical illustrations and a memoir by the Reverent Edmund F. Slafter, A.M., Boston, Prince Society, 1878-1882.

Sulte, Benjamin, 1841-1923. Royal Society of Canada, [n.p.] 1907

Gabriel Lalemant

Parkman, Francis. *The Jesuits in North America in the Seventeenth Century*, Boston, Little, Brown and Company, 1867

Kip, William Ingraham, bp., 1811-1893. *The Early Jesuit Missions in North America*, compiled and translated from the letters of the French Jesuits, with notes, New York, Wiley and Putnam, 1846.

Devine, E.J., 1860-1927. *Gabriel Lalemant: Victim of the Iroquois, 1610-1649*, Montréal, Canadian Messenger, 1916.

Ragueneau, Paul, 1608-1680. *Relation de ce qui s'est passé en la mission des pères de la Compagnie de Iesvs aux Hurons, pays de la Nouvelle France, és années 1648 & 1649*, Paris, Sébastien Cramoisy, imprimeur ordinaire du roy, & Gabriel Cramoisy, 1650.

Testore, Celestino, 1886-   *I santi martiri canado-americani della Compagnia di Gesù*, Isola del Liri, tip. A. Macioce & Pisani, 1930

Marguerite Bourgeoys

Simpson, Patricia, 1937-   *Marguerite Bourgeoys and Montréal, 1640-1665*, Montréal: McGill-Queens University Press, 1997

Doyle, Ignatius, Saint, Sister b. 1864. *Marguerite Bourgeoys and Her Congregation*, Gardenvale, Quebec, Garden City Press [c1940]

Atherton, William Henry, 1867-1950. *A Canadian Educationalist of the 17th Century, The Venerable Marguerite Bourgeoys, Foundress of the Congrégation de Notre-Dame (de Montréal),* pioneer social worker and teacher of Canada being an appreciation of her work on the occasion of her tercentennial anniversary (April 17, 1620-1700), S.I., s.n., 1920

Foran, Joseph K., 1857-1931. *Jeanne Mance: or "The Angel of the Colony," Foundress of the Hotel-Dieu Hospital, Montréal, pioneer nurse of North America, 1642-1673.*

Hale, Katherine. *Jeanne Mance*, Toronto, Ryerson Press c. 1930

Jean Talon

Chapais, Thomas. *The Great Intendant: A Chronicle of Jean Talon in Canada (1665-1672),* Toronto/Glasgow, Brook, 1914

Williams, Helen E. *Jean-Baptiste Talon*, Toronto: Ryerson Press [c. 1930]

Bissonnette, Réjeanne, 1943-   *Jean Talon et la Nouvelle-France*, Agincourt [Ont.]: Société canadienne du livre, 1985

Trout, Andrew P. *Jean-Baptiste Colbert*, Boston, Twayne Publications

Mims, Stewart Lea, 1880-   *Colbert's West India Policy*, New Haven, Yale University Press, 1912

Magdelaine de Verchères

Doughty, Arthur George (Sir). *A Daughter of New France, Being a Story of the Life and Times of Magdelaine de Verchères*, Ottawa, Mortimer Press, 1916

Brill, Ethel Claire. *Madeleine Takes Command*, Toronto, McGraw, 1946

Raymond, Ethel T. *Madeleine de Verchères*, Toronto: Ryerson Press c. 1928

Grant, Janet, 1957- *Madeleine de Verchères*, Toronto, Grolier, c. 1989

Le Sueur, William D., 1840-1917. *Count Frontenac*, London: Oxford University Press, 1926

Angélique Leblanc

Daigle, Jean, 1941- *Acadia of the Maritimes: Thematic Studies From the Beginning to the Present*, Université de Moncton, edited by Jean Daigle

Grand Pré Tragedy 1745-1755: The Noble Memorial [Nova Scotia: s.n. 19-]

Herbin, John Frederic. *Grand Pré*, Toronto, William Briggs, 1900

Longfellow, Henry Wadsworth, 1807-1882. *Evangeline, A Tale of Acadie*, London, Ward, Lock & Co., Limited, New York and Melbourne, edited by William Michael Rossetti, 1870.

Maillet, Antonine, et Scalabrini, Rita. *L'Acadie pour quasiment rien*, Montréal, Leméac, 1973

Lescarbot, Marc, 1570?-1630? *Nova Francia*, translated out of French into English by P.E.-, London: Printed by Andrew Hebb, and are to be sold at the signe of the Bell in Pauls Churchyard, [1625?]

Index